# Whispers of Kingston

## The Grave Whisperer, Volume 27

Angeline Gallant

Published by Luna Publishing, 2024.

While every precaution has been taken in the preparation of this book, the publisher assumes no responsibility for errors or omissions, or for damages resulting from the use of the information contained herein.

WHISPERS OF KINGSTON

**First edition. November 14, 2024.**



ISBN: 979-8230073543

Written by Angeline Gallant.

# Also by Angeline Gallant

**A Dragon's Diary**
Dreaming of Dragons

**Blood and Spirit Saga**
The Rising Wind

**Calling Her Heart**
Whisper of the Heart
No Turning Back
Forsake Me Not
Hear My Cry

**FORGET ME NOT**
Victoria, Ontario's Babies 1894 - 1895

**GENERATIONS OF THE VOLGA**
A Family's Legacy

**Guardian of the Heart**
Fallen Petals


**Keeper Of Secrets**
A Lady's Secret


**Kingston's Love Chronicles**
Springtime Promises


**Midnight's Awakening**
Heart of the Storm
Walking Through The Storm
Walking Through The Storm
Heart of the Storm


**Secrets of the Underworld**
Deklan's Dragons


**Tell My Story Collection**
Tell My Story: Germany 1851
Tell My Story: England 1852
Whispers From The Garrison Church

**The Wolf Whisperer Series**
Cry of a Warrior
Wolf Whisperer volumes 1 & 2
Endless White
The Wolf Whisperer volumes 1 & 2


**Timeless**
The Time Keeper's Sanctuary


**Timeless Whispers of Dervock Saga**
Secrets of Dervock


**Standalone**
Winds of Change vol 1-3


Watch for more at https://www.goodreads.com/author/show/19703964.Angeline_Gallant.

# Table of Contents

# CPL. UNKNOWN FORRESTER[1]

———

Cpl. Forrester's life in Kingston, Upper Canada, around 1783 would have been marked by the struggles and transitions faced by Loyalists and British soldiers who sought refuge in British North America after the American Revolutionary War. Kingston, a burgeoning military and Loyalist settlement, was a strategic hub. Known initially as Fort Frontenac, it attracted both military personnel and civilians seeking security in the shadow of the British garrison and the promise of land grants from the Crown.

As a corporal, Forrester would likely have served in a Loyalist regiment or a British regiment stationed in the region, possibly involved in fort-building and defensive preparations against the newly formed United States. Soldiers at this time often worked closely with newly arrived Loyalists, helping to secure supply lines, protect against Indigenous resistance due to growing settlement, and maintain British authority in an environment fraught with uncertainty.

Kingston was a rough and modest settlement in 1783. While St. Paul's Anglican Church, where he is buried, was a significant institution, it wasn't the stone structure seen today; the church's original wooden building was only erected a few years later in 1785. Life would have been simple and community-centered, with church services providing both religious guidance and a rare moment of social gathering.

The health challenges and harsh climate were likely major factors in his life. Soldiers of that era often faced malnutrition, poor shelter, and diseases like dysentery, smallpox, or pneumonia, which could quickly turn fatal. If he passed in service, he may have endured these hardships or injuries, dying as Kingston began to transform into a cornerstone of Loyalist life in Upper Canada.

---

HERE'S A GENEALOGY travel itinerary based on Cpl. Forrester's life in Kingston, Upper Canada, around 1783:

**Day 1: Arrival in Kingston**

• Morning: Arrive in Kingston and check into your accommodation.

• Afternoon: Visit Fort Henry National Historic Site. Explore the fortifications and learn about the military history of Kingston, including the role of British and Loyalist soldiers in the late 18th century

Fort Henry National Historic Site - Wikipedia[1]

• Evening: Enjoy dinner at a local restaurant and take a leisurely walk along the waterfront.

**Day 2: Exploring Loyalist History**

• Morning: Start your day with a visit to Bellevue House National Historic Site, the former home of Sir John A. Macdonald, to understand the broader context of Loyalist settlement in Upper Canada.

Kingston | The Canadian Encyclopedia[2]

• Afternoon: Head to St. Paul's Anglican Church and the Lower Burial Ground. Pay respects at the burial site of Cpl. Forrester and other early

---

1. https://en.wikipedia.org/wiki/Fort_Henry_National_Historic_Site

2. https://www.thecanadianencyclopedia.ca/en/article/kingston

settlers. Learn about the church's history and its significance to the community

RESOURCE[3]

RESOURCE[4]

---

• EVENING: ATTEND A historical walking tour of downtown Kingston, focusing on the Loyalist and military heritage of the area.

Day 3: Military and Community Life

• Morning: Visit the Military Communications and Electronics Museum to gain insights into the evolution of military technology and communication, which would have been crucial during Cpl. Forrester's time

A guide to museums & historic sites in Kingston[5]

---

• AFTERNOON: EXPLORE Kingston City Hall and the Customs House, landmarks that reflect the city's growth from a military outpost to a thriving community

Kingston | The Canadian Encyclopedia[6]

---

3. http://www.stpaulskingston.ca/history-of-st-pauls.htmlhttps://www.lowerburialground.ca/about/

4. http://www.stpaulskingston.ca/history-of-st-pauls.htmlhttps://www.lowerburialground.ca/about/

5. https://www.visitkingston.ca/a-guide-to-museums-historic-sites-in-kingston/

6. https://www.thecanadianencyclopedia.ca/en/article/kingston

• EVENING: RELAX WITH a boat tour of the Thousand Islands, offering a scenic view of the region that was once a strategic military area.

**Day 4: Nature and Reflection**

• Morning: Take a trip to Lemoine Point Conservation Area for a peaceful walk and reflection on the natural landscape that early settlers like Cpl. Forrester would have encountered.

• Afternoon: Visit the Murney Tower Museum, one of Kingston's Martello towers, to understand the defensive strategies employed during the 19th century

Kingston | The Canadian Encyclopedia[7]

---

• EVENING: CONCLUDE your trip with a visit to a local pub or café, reflecting on the journey and the historical insights gained.

This itinerary offers a blend of historical exploration, cultural immersion, and natural beauty, providing a comprehensive understanding of Cpl. Forrester's life and the early days of Kingston. Enjoy your trip!

---

7. https://www.thecanadianencyclopedia.ca/en/article/kingston

# CPL. UNKNOWN FORBES[2]

The burial of Cpl. Forbes in St. Paul's Anglican Churchyard, later encapsulated by the church's construction, gives us a poignant glimpse into Kingston's early Loyalist and military roots. By 1783, the town was largely a frontier settlement, with makeshift housing, sparse civilian infrastructure, and an influx of displaced Loyalists from the American colonies. Forbes's grave, later enveloped by St. Paul's Anglican Church, reflects the significance of his era's sacrifices and hardships, preserved in stone as Kingston evolved.

As a corporal in 1783, Forbes would have lived and likely died in an environment of disciplined resilience and camaraderie. Kingston was strategically vital; soldiers like Forbes would have known the land well, from the wooded wilderness surrounding the settlement to the water routes essential for trade, military strategy, and survival. The soldiers' daily lives were likely a mixture of guard duty, patrols, maintaining supplies, and physically demanding construction projects for the garrison and settlement.

While the Anglican Church was the established Church of England, soldiers and Loyalist settlers often faced harsh physical conditions that limited formal worship opportunities. In these early years, worship was likely conducted outdoors or in temporary structures, with Anglican clergy ministering to the military and scattered settlers, providing stability and hope to people whose worlds had been upended.

Cpl. Forbes's burial at St. Paul's shows that the church was not just a spiritual center but a testament to the community's resilience, marking the ground where their dead rested as sacred. As St. Paul's began to grow in importance, the fact that the church was later constructed over his resting place suggests how deeply these early soldiers were integrated into the fabric of Kingston's early society. His grave, resting beneath the eventual church floor, became part of the building's very foundation—symbolically reinforcing how Loyalist and British soldiers were quite literally the bedrock of Kingston's early development.

---

HERE'S A GENEALOGY travel itinerary based on the life and burial of Cpl. Forbes in Kingston, Upper Canada, around 1783:

**Day 1: Arrival and Introduction to Kingston**

• Morning: Arrive in Kingston and check into your accommodation.

• Afternoon: Visit Fort Henry National Historic Site to understand the military significance of Kingston during the late 18th century

Fort Henry National Historic Site - Wikipedia[1]

Explore the fortifications and learn about the daily lives of soldiers like Cpl. Forbes.

• Evening: Enjoy dinner at a local restaurant and take a leisurely walk along the waterfront, reflecting on the historical significance of the area.

**Day 2: Loyalist and Military Heritage**

• Morning: Start your day with a visit to Bellevue House National Historic Site, the former home of Sir John A. Macdonald, to gain insights into the Loyalist settlement in Upper Canada

A guide to museums & historic sites in Kingston[2]

---

1. https://en.wikipedia.org/wiki/Fort_Henry_National_Historic_Site

———————

• AFTERNOON: HEAD TO St. Paul's Anglican Church and the Lower Burial Ground. Pay respects at the burial site of Cpl. Forbes and other early settlers. Learn about the church's history and its role in the community

RESOURCE[3]

RESOURCE[4]

———————

• EVENING: ATTEND A historical walking tour of downtown Kingston, focusing on the Loyalist and military heritage of the area.

**Day 3: Exploring Early Kingston**

• Morning: Visit the Military Communications and Electronics Museum to gain insights into the evolution of military technology and communication, which would have been crucial during Cpl. Forbes's time.

List of National Historic Sites of Canada in Kingston, Ontario - Wikipedia[5]

———————

2. https://www.visitkingston.ca/a-guide-to-museums-historic-sites-in-kingston/

3. http://www.stpaulskingston.ca/history-of-st-pauls.htmlhttps://www.lowerburialground.ca/about/

4. http://www.stpaulskingston.ca/history-of-st-pauls.htmlhttps://www.lowerburialground.ca/about/

5. https://en.wikipedia.org/wiki/List_of_National_Historic_Sites_of_Canada_in_Kingston,_Ontario

• AFTERNOON: EXPLORE Kingston City Hall and the Customs House, landmarks that reflect the city's growth from a military outpost to a thriving community

RESOURCE[6]

———————

• EVENING: RELAX WITH a boat tour of the Thousand Islands, offering a scenic view of the region that was once a strategic military area.

**Day 4: Nature and Reflection**

• Morning: Take a trip to Lemoine Point Conservation Area for a peaceful walk and reflection on the natural landscape that early settlers like Cpl. Forbes would have encountered.

• Afternoon: Visit the Murney Tower Museum, one of Kingston's Martello towers, to understand the defensive strategies employed during the 19th century

RESOURCE[7]

———————

• EVENING: CONCLUDE your trip with a visit to a local pub or café, reflecting on the journey and the historical insights gained.

This itinerary offers a blend of historical exploration, cultural immersion, and natural beauty, providing a comprehensive understanding of Cpl. Forbes's life and the early days of Kingston. Enjoy your trip!

---

6. http://www.forthenry.com/

7. http://www.forthenry.com/

# UNKNOWN SWEENEY[3]

Unknown Sweeney's burial in St. Paul's Anglican Churchyard, which would later be built over, places him among the early military dead who are interwoven with Kingston's origins. His service in the 84th Regiment, also known as the Royal Highland Emigrants, aligns him with a distinguished Loyalist force formed during the American Revolutionary War to defend British interests in North America. This regiment was primarily composed of Scottish settlers, Loyalists, and Highlanders displaced by the conflict, and it included veterans of the Seven Years' War who remained fiercely loyal to Britain.

In 1783, Upper Canada was still largely a wild, unsettled frontier. For soldiers like Sweeney, who had already endured the Revolutionary War, life in Kingston could have felt both like a reprieve from battle and yet another trial. The men of the 84th, familiar with frontier life, would have found their skills in building, farming, and scouting in demand as they helped secure and develop British strongholds along the St. Lawrence River and Lake Ontario. Sweeney's duties likely included fortifying Kingston, providing a defensive buffer against potential American threats, and aiding in the integration of arriving Loyalist families.

Health conditions, however, were unforgiving. Disease and malnutrition plagued soldiers and settlers alike. Smallpox, fevers, dysentery, and other illnesses were common in crowded quarters with poor sanitation, especially during the brutal Canadian winters. Medical care was rudimentary, and survival often came down to resilience and fortune. The mortality rate was high, and it would not have been uncommon for men like Sweeney to die from complications of illness, injuries, or exposure rather than from combat.

When St. Paul's Anglican Church was later constructed over his grave, it was part of a tradition among settlers to honor the earliest and most loyal members of their community by keeping their burial sites close to, or even within, the walls of their most cherished buildings. Sweeney's resting place beneath the eventual church structure symbolized both his and his regiment's role in the very bones of Kingston's establishment. His burial, along with others of the 84th and the early Loyalists, infused St. Paul's Anglican Church with the spirit and sacrifice of these early defenders. Each time parishioners entered for worship, they were reminded of those, like Sweeney, whose service in the regiment ensured Kingston's survival and paved the way for the fledgling community's future.

Today, Sweeney's hidden grave and those of his comrades in arms continue to embody the deep-rooted connection between Kingston's military and Loyalist origins. Their presence beneath the church, though hidden, persists as a testament to a chapter of hardship, loyalty, and endurance that set the foundations of Upper Canada itself.

———————

HERE'S A GENEALOGY travel itinerary based on the life and burial of Unknown Sweeney in Kingston, Upper Canada, around 1783:

**Day 1: Arrival and Introduction to Kingston**

• Morning: Arrive in Kingston and check into your accommodation.

• Afternoon: Visit Fort Henry National Historic Site to understand the military significance of Kingston during the late 18th century

Ontario Loyalist Records • FamilySearch[1]

Explore the fortifications and learn about the daily lives of soldiers like Sweeney.

• Evening: Enjoy dinner at a local restaurant and take a leisurely walk along the waterfront, reflecting on the historical significance of the area.

**Day 2: Loyalist and Military Heritage**

• Morning: Start your day with a visit to Bellevue House National Historic Site, the former home of Sir John A. Macdonald, to gain insights into the Loyalist settlement in Upper Canada

84th Regiment of Foot (Royal Highland Emigrants) - Wikipedia[2]

• AFTERNOON: HEAD TO St. Paul's Anglican Church and the Lower Burial Ground. Pay respects at the burial site of Unknown Sweeney and other early settlers. Learn about the church's history and its role in the community

RESOURCE[3]

• EVENING: ATTEND A historical walking tour of downtown Kingston, focusing on the Loyalist and military heritage of the area.

**Day 3: Exploring Early Kingston**

1. https://www.familysearch.org/en/wiki/Ontario_Loyalist_Records

2. https://en.wikipedia.org/wiki/84th_Regiment_of_Foot_%28Royal_Highland_Emigrants%29

3. https://www.canlii.org/w/canlii/1995CanLIIDocs136.pdfhttps://www.lowerburialground.ca/burials/military-and-black-interments/

- Morning: Visit the Military Communications and Electronics Museum to gain insights into the evolution of military technology and communication, which would have been crucial during Sweeney's time

RESOURCE[4].

---

- AFTERNOON: EXPLORE Kingston City Hall and the Customs House, landmarks that reflect the city's growth from a military outpost to a thriving community

RESOURCE[5]

---

- EVENING: RELAX WITH a boat tour of the Thousand Islands, offering a scenic view of the region that was once a strategic military area.

**Day 4: Nature and Reflection**

- Morning: Take a trip to Lemoine Point Conservation Area for a peaceful walk and reflection on the natural landscape that early settlers like Sweeney would have encountered.

- Afternoon: Visit the Murney Tower Museum, one of Kingston's Martello towers, to understand the defensive strategies employed during the 19th century

RESOURCE[6]

---

4. https://kids.kiddle.co/84th_Regiment_of_Foot_%28Royal_Highland_Emigrants%29

5. https://military-history.fandom.com/wiki/
   84th_Regiment_of_Foot_%28Royal_Highland_Emigrants%29

6. https://military-history.fandom.com/wiki/
   84th_Regiment_of_Foot_%28Royal_Highland_Emigrants%29

• EVENING: CONCLUDE your trip with a visit to a local pub or café, reflecting on the journey and the historical insights gained.

This itinerary offers a blend of historical exploration, cultural immersion, and natural beauty, providing a comprehensive understanding of Unknown Sweeney's life and the early days of Kingston. Enjoy your trip!

# JOANNA (BEASLEY) CARTWRIGHT[4]

Joanna Beasley's birth in Albany, New York, on March 9, 1726, places her squarely within a period of growth, frontier resilience, and complex cultural exchanges. Albany in the early 18th century was a bustling Dutch-influenced settlement and one of the most significant centers in the English colonies for trade, especially in fur and other goods exchanged with Indigenous nations.

Albany's position along the Hudson River made it a vital gateway for both commerce and diplomacy between English settlers, Dutch residents, and Indigenous nations such as the Mohawk and other Haudenosaunee (Iroquois) Confederacy members. The Beasley family would have witnessed regular gatherings of traders, Native Americans, and European settlers, each adding their language, customs, and goods to the lively markets and meeting grounds. Joanna likely grew up hearing a mixture of English and Dutch spoken in homes and public spaces, with the distinct sounds of Indigenous languages woven into the background.

By 1726, Albany was under English governance, but the Dutch influence remained strong in architecture, religion, and daily life. Homes were often built in the sturdy, steep-roofed Dutch style, and family life was heavily centered around the Dutch Reformed Church, which likely played a major role in Joanna's upbringing. Sundays would have been strictly observed, with most families attending lengthy church services and observing the Sabbath with family meals and gatherings.

Her father, John "James" Francis Beasley, would have been a man of some resilience and adaptability, navigating the shifting power dynamics between the Dutch, the English, and the Native Americans. Whether he was involved in trade, craftsmanship, or agriculture, he would have had to manage interactions across these diverse cultures, often working within Albany's evolving laws under English rule.

Women in Albany during this period, including Joanna's mother, Lydia Dally, led lives both constrained and empowered by necessity. They managed the household and were responsible for tasks like cooking, sewing, and tending to livestock if the family had any. Lydia would have raised Joanna with a deep knowledge of household management and possibly some business skills, as it wasn't uncommon for Albany women to run family shops or inns when their husbands were absent. Life was physically demanding—heating, cooking, and washing required labor-intensive processes. Clothing was handmade, and even daily meals involved substantial preparation.

Albany in the 1720s was, however, not without its dangers. Relations between the English settlers and the Indigenous nations were often uneasy. Although Albany maintained relatively stable diplomatic ties with its Native American neighbors, families would have been alert to news of skirmishes or shifts in alliances. Joanna's parents would have been especially aware of their ties to England as tensions began to simmer between colonial authorities and Indigenous groups over land, trade rights, and resources.

Children like Joanna grew up in this complex setting, blending elements of Dutch, English, and Indigenous cultures in their daily lives. Education was informal, often revolving around religious instruction, household skills, and, if a family was literate, reading from the Bible or Dutch storybooks. As a girl, Joanna's formal education would have been limited compared to boys', though she would likely have been taught to read enough to engage in religious study.

In this setting, Joanna's early years would have been marked by close-knit family relationships, religious observance, and the demands of frontier life. Though Albany in 1726 was a small town by modern standards, it was a vibrant, multi-ethnic hub where the convergence of European and Indigenous cultures created a unique environment for a girl like Joanna to grow up in—a world where history was unfolding at every turn along the Hudson River.

———

HERE'S A GENEALOGY travel itinerary based on Joanna Beasley's birth and early life in Albany, New York, in 1726:

———

**DAY 1: ARRIVAL AND Introduction to Colonial Albany**

Morning:

• Arrival in Albany, New York: Check into your accommodation. Recommended: Albany Hilton for its central location.

• Welcome Breakfast: Enjoy a traditional breakfast at the hotel and meet your genealogy guide.

Afternoon:

• Orientation Session: Visit the New York State Library to learn about the resources available for genealogical research, including family genealogies, local histories, and church records

Genealogy Research in Albany Trip | NYG&B[1]

---

EVENING:

• Dinner: Dine at The Olde English Pub and Pantry, located in the historic Quackenbush Square

Research in Albany | New York Genealogical & Biographical Society[2]

DAY 2: EXPLORING DUTCH Heritage and Daily Life

**Morning:**

• Crailo State Historic Site: Visit this museum to learn about early Dutch settlers and see the interior of a traditional Dutch home

3 Road Trip Itineraries for Albany County, New York[3]

• FIRST CHURCH IN ALBANY: Explore the oldest church in Albany, established in 1642, and its rich history

Itinerary Albany: Your Quick Guide to Exploring the City[4]

AFTERNOON:

• Lunch: Enjoy a meal at Iron Gate Café, featuring recipes from the colonial era.

---

2. https://www.newyorkfamilyhistory.org/events/research-albany

3. https://www.albany.org/blog/post/road-trip-itineraries-for-albany-county/

4. https://familydestinationsguide.com/itinerary-albany/

- Historical Walking Tour: Take a guided tour of Albany to see historical landmarks and learn about daily life in the 1720s

RESOURCE[5]

---

EVENING:

- Lecture on Colonial Life: Attend a lecture on the social and cultural aspects of life in Albany during the early 18th century

Hudson River Trading[6]

---

## DAY 3: RESEARCH AND Cultural Exchanges

**Morning:**

- Genealogical Research: Spend the morning at the New York State Archives in Albany, researching state records, including birth, marriage, and land records

Genealogy Research in Albany Trip | NYG&B[7]

---

AFTERNOON:

- Albany Institute of History & Art: Visit this museum to explore exhibits on Albany's colonial history and art

Hudson's Bay Company | The Canadian Encyclopedia[8]

---


5. https://bing.com/search?q=Hudson+River+trade+18th+century&form=SKPBOT

6. https://www.hudsonrivertrading.com/

7. https://www.newyorkfamilyhistory.org/events/albany-genealogy-research-trip

8. https://www.thecanadianencyclopedia.ca/en/article/hudsons-bay-company

---

• LUNCH: HAVE LUNCH at Jack's Oyster House, a historic Albany restaurant.

Evening:

• Community Gathering: Join a local community gathering to share stories and learn about the social fabric of colonial life

Fur Trade Route Networks | The Canadian Encyclopedia[9]

---

## DAY 4: HISTORICAL CONTEXT and Personal Reflection

**Morning:**

• Hudson River Trade and Diplomacy: Visit sites along the Hudson River to understand its role in trade and diplomacy between English settlers, Dutch residents, and Indigenous nations

Hudson River Cargoes and Carriers[10]

Genealogy Research in Albany Trip | NYG&B[11]

Research in Albany | New York Genealogical & Biographical Society[12]

---

• FORT ORANGE: EXPLORE the site of the original Dutch settlement and learn about its significance in Albany's history

---

9. https://www.thecanadianencyclopedia.ca/en/article/fur-trade-routes

10. https://www.hrmm.org/history-blog/hudson-river-cargoes-and-carriers

11. https://www.newyorkfamilyhistory.org/events/albany-genealogy-research-trip

12. https://www.newyorkfamilyhistory.org/events/research-albany

8.4 Commerce, Collusion, and Conflict in the 18th Century –
Canadian History: Pre-Confederation[13].

---

AFTERNOON:

• Lunch: Enjoy a meal at The Hollow Bar + Kitchen.

• Interactive History Session: Participate in a reenactment or
interactive session about life during the early 18th century and the
cultural exchanges in Albany

RESOURCE[14]

---

EVENING:

• Reflection and Discussion: Reflect on the day's experiences and
discuss the impact of cultural exchanges on Joanna's life over dinner at
Wellington's in the Renaissance Albany Hotel

First Church in Albany[15]

---

**DAY 5: DEPARTURE AND Final Research**

**Morning:**

• Final Research Session: Return to the New York State Library or
Archives for any last-minute research.

---

13. https://opentextbc.ca/preconfederation/chapter/8-4-commerce-collusion-and-conflict-in-the-
    18th-century/

14. https://bing.com/search?q=Dutch+Reformed+Church+Albany+history&form=SKPBOT

15. https://www.firstchurchinalbany.org/

• Farewell Brunch: Have a farewell brunch with your group at Wellington's in the Renaissance Albany Hotel.

Afternoon:

• Departure: Check out of your hotel and depart Albany with a deeper understanding of your family's history and the colonial era.

———

FEEL FREE TO ADJUST the itinerary based on your interests and research needs. Enjoy your genealogical journey in Albany!

———

JOANNA'S CHRISTENING on March 13, 1726, just four days after her birth, reflects the importance of baptism in early colonial life and the strong influence of the Reformed Dutch Church in Albany. In this close-knit, faith-centered community, baptisms were significant milestones celebrated not just by immediate family but often by the entire congregation. Albany's residents regarded christening as essential for welcoming a child into the community and the faith, a practice with both spiritual and social implications.

The baptismal ceremony, likely held in the Dutch Reformed Church, would have been a solemn occasion. The church itself would have been modest but well-cared-for, constructed with traditional Dutch architectural features—thick walls, arched windows, and a steeply sloped roof. The interior was likely simple, with wooden pews and a central pulpit, placing the focus on worship and community rather than decoration.

Joanna's parents, John "James" Francis Beasley and Lydia Dally, would have dressed in their best clothes for the event, a reflection of the day's significance. Baptisms were also social occasions where Albany families connected and reaffirmed ties within their community. It's possible that family friends or prominent community members were chosen as Joanna's godparents. This role was often assigned to trusted friends or relatives, creating lasting bonds that reinforced the supportive, interdependent nature of colonial society. Godparents were seen as spiritual guides and protectors, committed to helping the parents raise the child in the faith.

Following the ceremony, it was common for families to host a modest gathering. Though Albany wasn't a wealthy community, there may have been a small reception at the family's home or with neighbors, involving bread, cheese, and perhaps a bit of local ale or cider if they had the means. Neighbors might bring simple gifts or blessings for the child, and Joanna's baptism day would have been one of the first community gatherings she experienced.

The Dutch Reformed Church, which held sway in Albany at the time, emphasized a strict, Calvinist approach to life. The church's teachings stressed discipline, family duty, and respect for social order. These values would shape Joanna's upbringing. Her early baptism signaled her formal entrance into a life guided by these principles and into a community that saw itself as part of God's chosen people in a new world.

For Joanna, her christening marked the beginning of a life grounded in faith, family, and the close communal bonds of Albany. She would grow up within a world where church services and religious milestones punctuated the rhythms of daily life. Baptisms, weddings, and funerals were not only personal rites but events that bound the townspeople together, fostering a shared identity that helped Albany's settlers face the challenges of life on the colonial frontier.

HERE'S A GENEALOGY travel itinerary based on Joanna's christening and early life in Albany, New York, in 1726:

---

## DAY 1: ARRIVAL AND Introduction to Colonial Albany

Morning:

• Arrival in Albany, New York: Check into your accommodation. Recommended: Albany Hilton for its central location.

• Welcome Breakfast: Enjoy a traditional breakfast at the hotel and meet your genealogy guide.

Afternoon:

• Orientation Session: Visit the New York State Library to learn about the resources available for genealogical research, including family genealogies, local histories, and church records

Genealogy Research in Albany Trip | NYG&B[16]

---

EVENING:

• Dinner: Dine at The Olde English Pub and Pantry, located in the historic Quackenbush Square

Research in Albany (Spring) | New York Genealogical & Biographical Society[17]

---

## DAY 2: EXPLORING DUTCH Heritage and Baptism Traditions

16. https://www.newyorkfamilyhistory.org/events/albany-genealogy-research-trip

17. https://www.newyorkfamilyhistory.org/events/research-albany-spring

**Morning:**

• First Church in Albany: Visit the oldest church in Albany, established in 1642, to understand its role in Joanna's christening and the community's religious life

3 Road Trip Itineraries for Albany County, New York[18]

———————

• CRAILO STATE HISTORIC Site: Explore this museum to learn about early Dutch settlers and see the interior of a traditional Dutch home

Itinerary Albany: Your Quick Guide to Exploring the City[19]

———————

AFTERNOON:

• Lunch: Enjoy a meal at Iron Gate Café, featuring recipes from the colonial era.

• Historical Walking Tour: Take a guided tour of Albany to see historical landmarks and learn about daily life in the 1720s

Welcome To The Colonial Albany Project Website[20]

———————

EVENING:

• Lecture on Colonial Life: Attend a lecture on the social and cultural aspects of life in Albany during the early 18th century

---

18. https://www.albany.org/blog/post/road-trip-itineraries-for-albany-county/

19. https://familydestinationsguide.com/itinerary-albany/

20. https://exhibitions.nysm.nysed.gov/albany/welcome.html

About The Colonial Albany Social History Project[21]

---

**DAY 3: RESEARCH AND Community Connections**

**Morning:**

• Genealogical Research: Spend the morning at the New York State Archives in Albany, researching state records, including birth, marriage, and land records

Genealogy Research in Albany Trip | NYG&B[22]

---

AFTERNOON:

• Albany Institute of History & Art: Visit this museum to explore exhibits on Albany's colonial history and art

Friends and Enemies[23]

---

• LUNCH: HAVE LUNCH at Jack's Oyster House, a historic Albany restaurant.

Evening:

• Community Gathering: Join a local community gathering to share stories and learn about the social fabric of colonial life

RESOURCE[24]

---

21. https://exhibitions.nysm.nysed.gov/albany/whoarewe.html

22. https://www.newyorkfamilyhistory.org/events/albany-genealogy-research-trip

23. https://exhibitions.nysm.nysed.gov/albany/friends.html

24. https://bing.com/search?q=Albany+Dutch+Reformed+Church+history&form=SKPBOT

## DAY 4: HISTORICAL CONTEXT and Personal Reflection

**Morning:**

• Hudson River Trade and Diplomacy: Visit sites along the Hudson River to understand its role in trade and diplomacy between English settlers, Dutch residents, and Indigenous nations

First Church in Albany[25]

Genealogy Research in Albany Trip | NYG&B[26]

Research in Albany (Spring) | New York Genealogical & Biographical Society[27]

• FORT ORANGE: EXPLORE the site of the original Dutch settlement and learn about its significance in Albany's history

First Church in Albany (Reformed) - Wikipedia[28]

AFTERNOON:

• Lunch: Enjoy a meal at The Hollow Bar + Kitchen.

• Interactive History Session: Participate in a reenactment or interactive session about life during the early 18th century and the cultural exchanges in Albany

---

25. https://www.firstchurchinalbany.org/

26. https://www.newyorkfamilyhistory.org/events/albany-genealogy-research-trip

27. https://www.newyorkfamilyhistory.org/events/research-albany-spring

28. https://en.wikipedia.org/wiki/First_Church_in_Albany_%28Reformed%29

<u>Dutch Reformed Church In Albany, New York</u>[29]

—————

EVENING:

• Reflection and Discussion: Reflect on the day's experiences and discuss the impact of cultural exchanges on Joanna's life over dinner at Wellington's in the Renaissance Albany Hotel

<u>Manuscript Registers—Baptisms and Marriages</u>[30]

—————

## DAY 5: DEPARTURE AND Final Research

**Morning:**

• Final Research Session: Return to the New York State Library or Archives for any last-minute research.

• Farewell Brunch: Have a farewell brunch with your group at Wellington's in the Renaissance Albany Hotel.

Afternoon:

• Departure: Check out of your hotel and depart Albany with a deeper understanding of your family's history and the colonial era.

—————

FEEL FREE TO ADJUST the itinerary based on your interests and research needs. Enjoy your genealogical journey in Albany!

—————

29. https://exhibitions.nysm.nysed.gov/albany/drc.html

30. https://www.firstchurchinalbany.org/manuscript-registersmdashbaptisms-and-marriages.html

WHEN JOANNA WAS AROUND 12 years old, the Methodist movement began in England in the 1730s, under the leadership of John and Charles Wesley. Though it would take some years for Methodism to establish itself in the American colonies, its founding was a sign of the broader religious shifts occurring in the Atlantic world, part of a wave of new religious thought and revivalism that would soon touch communities like Albany.

While Joanna's early religious life was shaped by the Dutch Reformed Church's strict Calvinism, she and her family may have heard of Methodist ideas as they spread from England to the colonies. Methodism emphasized personal faith, moral discipline, and a "methodical" approach to spiritual practice, offering a different approach to worship than the hierarchical, sermon-focused style of her church. Though Methodism didn't immediately influence her community, the growth of this movement—and others like it—would eventually shape religious dynamics in America.

By the time Methodism began reaching colonial towns in earnest in the 1740s and 1750s, Joanna would have been a young adult, perhaps already married or starting her own family. As a resident of Albany, she would have likely noticed the effects of the First Great Awakening, a Protestant revival that spread across the colonies in the late 1730s and 1740s. Preachers like George Whitefield traveled widely, attracting crowds and challenging the rigid religious structures that Joanna had grown up with. This religious fervor encouraged a more emotional and personal relationship with faith, drawing people of various social and ethnic backgrounds.

In Albany, this religious wave would have likely stirred curiosity, skepticism, and even opposition among the established Dutch Reformed Church members. Albany's religious elders, steeped in the traditions of the Reformed Church, might have viewed the emotional, revivalist style of the Great Awakening preachers as unsettling or even disruptive. However, some younger or more open-minded members of the community may have felt intrigued by these new spiritual expressions.

For Joanna, living through this era meant witnessing a growing diversity of beliefs and practices. The Methodist and Great Awakening movements marked the beginning of a religious landscape that valued personal conviction and questioned traditional authority—ideas that would subtly, but steadily, begin to reshape colonial American identity. While she may have continued in her Dutch Reformed faith, Joanna's community was gradually exposed to new religious influences, broadening the range of faith traditions that would ultimately flourish in the New World.

The spiritual undercurrents of the Methodist movement and the Great Awakening marked a departure from the orthodoxy she was raised in, signaling a more diverse future for faith in America. As Albany continued to grow, religious pluralism would become an increasingly familiar part of Joanna's world, setting the stage for the evolving spiritual dynamics of her children's and grandchildren's generations.

---

HERE'S A GENEALOGY travel itinerary based on Joanna's experience with the early religious shifts in Albany, New York, during the 1730s and 1740s:

---

**DAY 1: ARRIVAL AND Introduction to Colonial Albany**

Morning:

• Arrival in Albany, New York: Check into your accommodation. Recommended: Albany Hilton for its central location.

• Welcome Breakfast: Enjoy a traditional breakfast at the hotel and meet your genealogy guide.

Afternoon:

• Orientation Session: Visit the New York State Library to learn about the resources available for genealogical research, including family genealogies, local histories, and church records

The Urban Threshold and the Second Great Awakening: Revivalism in New York State, 1825-1835[31]

---

EVENING:

• Dinner: Dine at The Olde English Pub and Pantry, located in the historic Quackenbush Square

First Great Awakening, Summary, Facts, Significance[32]

---

**DAY 2: EXPLORING DUTCH Heritage and Early Methodism**

Morning:

• First Church in Albany: Visit the oldest church in Albany, established in 1642, to understand its role in Joanna's early religious life and the community's religious practices

---

31. https://www.jstor.org/stable/40959057

32. https://www.americanhistorycentral.com/entries/first-great-awakening/

<u>Awakenings in the Burned-Over District: New Light on the Historical Setting of the First Vision | Religious Studies Center</u>[33]

---

• CRAILO STATE HISTORIC Site: Explore this museum to learn about early Dutch settlers and see the interior of a traditional Dutch home

<u>Great Awakening - First, Second & Definition | HISTORY</u>[34]

---

AFTERNOON:

• Lunch: Enjoy a meal at Iron Gate Café, featuring recipes from the colonial era.

• Historical Walking Tour: Take a guided tour of Albany to see historical landmarks and learn about daily life in the 1730s and 1740s

<u>First Great Awakening - Wikipedia</u>[35]

---

EVENING:

• Lecture on Colonial Life: Attend a lecture on the social and cultural aspects of life in Albany during the early 18th century

<u>RESOURCE</u>[36]

---

33. https://rsc.byu.edu/exploring-first-vision/awakenings-burned-over-district-new-light-historical-setting-first-vision

34. https://www.history.com/topics/european-history/great-awakening

35. https://en.wikipedia.org/wiki/First_Great_Awakening

36. https://www.nyac.com/files/archives/250th+anniversary/timeline/2016-nyac-archives-banner-small-2016_09_16.pdf

---

## DAY 3: RESEARCH AND Religious Shifts

**Morning:**

• Genealogical Research: Spend the morning at the New York State Archives in Albany, researching state records, including birth, marriage, and land records

The Urban Threshold and the Second Great Awakening: Revivalism in New York State, 1825-1835[37]

---

## AFTERNOON:

• Albany Institute of History & Art: Visit this museum to explore exhibits on Albany's colonial history and art

Methodist church in Albany[38]

---

• LUNCH: HAVE LUNCH at Jack's Oyster House, a historic Albany restaurant.

Evening:

• Community Gathering: Join a local community gathering to share stories and learn about the social fabric of colonial life

The Power of Religious Activism in Tocqueville's America: The Second Great Awakening and the Rise of Temperance and Abolitionism in New York State | Social Science History | Cambridge Core[39]

---

37. https://www.jstor.org/stable/40959057

38. https://exhibitions.nysm.nysed.gov/albany/org/meth.html

## DAY 4: HISTORICAL CONTEXT and Personal Reflection

**Morning:**

The Urban Threshold and the Second Great Awakening: Revivalism in New York State, 1825-1835[40]

First Great Awakening, Summary, Facts, Significance[41]

• HUDSON RIVER TRADE and Diplomacy: Visit sites along the Hudson River to understand its role in trade and diplomacy between English settlers, Dutch residents, and Indigenous nations

Dutch Reformed Church In Albany, New York[42]

• FORT ORANGE: EXPLORE the site of the original Dutch settlement and learn about its significance in Albany's history

Records of the Reformed Dutch Church of Albany, New York, 1683–1809[43]

AFTERNOON:

---

39. https://www.cambridge.org/core/journals/social-science-history/article/power-of-religious-activism-in-tocquevilles-america-the-second-great-awakening-and-the-rise-of-temperance-and-abolitionism-in-new-york-state/8769D5957684002ED8B5DCE6667B6B38

40. https://www.jstor.org/stable/40959057

41. https://www.americanhistorycentral.com/entries/first-great-awakening/

42. https://exhibitions.nysm.nysed.gov/albany/drc.html

43. https://mathcs.clarku.edu/~djoyce/gen/albany/refchurch.html

• Lunch: Enjoy a meal at The Hollow Bar + Kitchen.

• Interactive History Session: Participate in a reenactment or interactive session about life during the early 18th century and the cultural exchanges in Albany

The Dutch Reformed in North America | Tabletalk[44]

---

EVENING:

• Reflection and Discussion: Reflect on the day's experiences and discuss the impact of cultural exchanges on Joanna's life over dinner at Wellington's in the Renaissance Albany Hotel

Churches of early Albany[45]

---

**DAY 5: DEPARTURE AND Final Research**

Morning:

• Final Research Session: Return to the New York State Library or Archives for any last-minute research.

• Farewell Brunch: Have a farewell brunch with your group at Wellington's in the Renaissance Albany Hotel.

Afternoon:

• Departure: Check out of your hotel and depart Albany with a deeper understanding of your family's history and the colonial era.

---

44. https://tabletalkmagazine.com/article/2019/01/dutch-reformed-north-america/

45. https://exhibitions.nysm.nysed.gov/albany/churches.html

FEEL FREE TO ADJUST the itinerary based on your interests and research needs. Enjoy your genealogical journey in Albany!

---

AT JUST 16, JOANNA Beasley married Richard Cartwright I on July 12, 1747, in Albany, New York. Marrying at such a young age was typical for the time, especially in a community where family ties, trade, and alliances were crucial to social stability. Richard Cartwright, like Joanna, was likely a prominent member of Albany's community, with ambitions in trade or land acquisition—a pursuit that would become increasingly vital as Albany's economy developed.

Their marriage ceremony would have been held either at the Dutch Reformed Church or at home, surrounded by family, friends, and neighbors. This wedding, especially within the Albany community, was not just a personal commitment but a public declaration of loyalty to family and faith. As a new wife, Joanna would have taken on substantial responsibilities, overseeing household tasks, helping her husband in trade if needed, and managing the home's finances if she was literate and capable, which was common in Dutch families. She would also be expected to bear and raise children, a role seen as essential to building the future of both her family and the community.

The Cartwrights' early years of marriage in Albany would have been marked by the rhythms of colonial life—trading seasons, church gatherings, and occasional news from the outside world. Albany's strategic location along the Hudson River would have meant that Richard, if he was involved in trade, often had dealings with other colonial settlements and perhaps even contacts in Canada or overseas. Trade with Indigenous groups, especially in fur and other goods, would have been an integral part of their life, requiring a careful balance of trust, negotiation, and respect for local Indigenous nations.

However, these early years would not have been without challenges. Albany in the mid-18th century was still a frontier town, vulnerable to conflicts as colonial powers vied for control of North America. Tensions between the French and British, as well as hostilities involving Indigenous allies, meant that towns like Albany were periodically on edge, worried about raids or shifting alliances. This environment required resilience and a readiness to adapt, qualities that Joanna likely embodied as she settled into her role as a wife and, soon, a mother.

The Cartwrights may also have experienced, or at least heard about, the increasing influence of the Great Awakening as it spread into the northern colonies. The religious revival movement encouraged a more personal approach to faith, one that differed from the formal, ritual-driven practices of the Dutch Reformed Church. As a young woman, Joanna may have been curious about these new ideas or, conversely, might have found comfort in the stability of her established religious tradition. Either way, she would have been aware of the changing tides, witnessing how faith was beginning to become a deeply personal choice, not merely a matter of heritage.

In the first few years of her marriage, Joanna would have started building a household that aligned with both Cartwright family traditions and her Dutch heritage, weaving together the customs she inherited from her parents. Each season would have brought its own demands: summer for growing and preserving food, fall for trading and preparing for winter, and winter for hunkering down against the harsh Albany cold.

In this new phase of her life, Joanna's days were likely filled with learning how to manage a home and developing the resilience needed to navigate the complexities of frontier life with her husband, Richard. Their marriage not only marked the beginning of their partnership but also their entry into the intricate network of families, trade alliances, and community bonds that defined Albany's colonial society.

---

HERE'S A GENEALOGY travel itinerary based on Joanna Beasley's marriage to Richard Cartwright I in Albany, New York, in 1747:

---

## DAY 1: ARRIVAL AND Introduction to Colonial Albany

Morning:

• Arrival in Albany, New York: Check into your accommodation. Recommended: Albany Hilton for its central location.

• Welcome Breakfast: Enjoy a traditional breakfast at the hotel and meet your genealogy guide.

Afternoon:

• Orientation Session: Visit the New York State Library to learn about the resources available for genealogical research, including family genealogies, local histories, and church records

History of the Hudson River - Wikipedia[46]

---

EVENING:

• Dinner: Dine at The Olde English Pub and Pantry, located in the historic Quackenbush Square

The Worlds of the Seventeenth-Century Hudson Valley - New York Almanack[47]

---

46. https://en.wikipedia.org/wiki/History_of_the_Hudson_River

---

## DAY 2: EXPLORING DUTCH Heritage and Marriage Traditions

Morning:

• First Church in Albany: Visit the oldest church in Albany, established in 1642, to understand its role in Joanna's marriage and the community's religious practices

<u>5.7 The Five Nations: War, Population, and Diplomacy – Canadian History: Pre-Confederation</u>[48]

---

• CRAILO STATE HISTORIC Site: Explore this museum to learn about early Dutch settlers and see the interior of a traditional Dutch home

<u>Albany Plan of Union, Summary, Facts, Significance, APUSH</u>[49]

---

AFTERNOON:

• Lunch: Enjoy a meal at Iron Gate Café, featuring recipes from the colonial era.

• Historical Walking Tour: Take a guided tour of Albany to see historical landmarks and learn about daily life in the 1740s

<u>Reasons and Motives for the Albany Plan of Union, [July 1754]</u>[50]

---

47. https://www.newyorkalmanack.com/2014/06/the-worlds-of-the-seventeenth-century-hudson-valley/

48. https://opentextbc.ca/preconfederation2e/chapter/5-7-the-five-nations-war-population-and-diplomacy/

49. https://www.americanhistorycentral.com/entries/albany-plan-of-union/

EVENING:

• Lecture on Colonial Life: Attend a lecture on the social and cultural aspects of life in Albany during the mid-18th century

RESOURCE[51].

DAY 3: RESEARCH AND Trade in Colonial Albany

Morning:

• Genealogical Research: Spend the morning at the New York State Archives in Albany, researching state records, including birth, marriage, and land records

History of the Hudson River - Wikipedia[52]

AFTERNOON:

• Albany Institute of History & Art: Visit this museum to explore exhibits on Albany's colonial history and art

An Early Albany Girlhood[53]

---

50. https://founders.archives.gov/documents/Franklin/01-05-02-0109

51. https://www.cambridge.org/core/services/aop-cambridge-core/content/view/

3AADF08B3BB0A7AADFF80EB6E2D55DC2/S0021937122002295a.pdf/

confederal_union_and_empire_placing_the_albany_plan_1754_in_imperial_context.pdf

52. https://en.wikipedia.org/wiki/History_of_the_Hudson_River

53. https://exhibitions.nysm.nysed.gov/albany/pgms/women.html

• LUNCH: HAVE LUNCH at Jack's Oyster House, a historic Albany restaurant.

Evening:

• Community Gathering: Join a local community gathering to share stories and learn about the social fabric of colonial life

A Woman of Business - Women & the American Story[54]

---

## DAY 4: HISTORICAL CONTEXT and Personal Reflection

Morning:

https://en.wikipedia.org/wiki/History_of_the_Hudson_River

The Worlds of the Seventeenth-Century Hudson Valley - New York Almanack[55]

---

• HUDSON RIVER TRADE and Diplomacy: Visit sites along the Hudson River to understand its role in trade and diplomacy between English settlers, Dutch residents, and Indigenous nations

English Colonies - Women & the American Story[56]

---

54. https://wams.nyhistory.org/settler-colonialism-and-revolution/settler-colonialism/woman-of-business/

55. https://www.newyorkalmanack.com/2014/06/the-worlds-of-the-seventeenth-century-hudson-valley/

56. https://wams.nyhistory.org/early-encounters/english-colonies/

• FORT ORANGE: EXPLORE the site of the original Dutch settlement and learn about its significance in Albany's history

<u>RESOURCE</u>[57]

---

AFTERNOON:

• Lunch: Enjoy a meal at The Hollow Bar + Kitchen.

• Interactive History Session: Participate in a reenactment or interactive session about life during the mid-18th century and the cultural exchanges in Albany

<u>Records of the Reformed Dutch Church of Albany, New York, 1683–1809</u>[58]

---

EVENING:

• Reflection and Discussion: Reflect on the day's experiences and discuss the impact of cultural exchanges on Joanna's life over dinner at Wellington's in the Renaissance Albany Hotel

<u>Manuscript Registers—Baptisms and Marriages</u>[59]

---

**DAY 5: DEPARTURE AND Final Research**

---

57. https://bing.com/

    search?q=Dutch+Reformed+Church+marriage+traditions+1747+Albany+New+York&form

    =SKPBOT

58. https://mathcs.clarku.edu/~djoyce/gen/albany/refchurch.html

59. https://www.firstchurchinalbany.org/manuscript-registersmdashbaptisms-and-marriages.html

Morning:

• Final Research Session: Return to the New York State Library or Archives for any last-minute research.

• Farewell Brunch: Have a farewell brunch with your group at Wellington's in the Renaissance Albany Hotel.

Afternoon:

• Departure: Check out of your hotel and depart Albany with a deeper understanding of your family's history and the colonial era.

———————

FEEL FREE TO ADJUST the itinerary based on your interests and research needs. Enjoy your genealogical journey in Albany!

———————

AT 21, JOANNA WELCOMED her first child, John, on July 12, 1747, in Albany—the same day she and Richard had celebrated their fifth wedding anniversary. His birth would have been a milestone, not only marking Joanna's entrance into motherhood but also further solidifying the Cartwright family's place in Albany's social fabric. In a community that valued family legacy, John's arrival would have carried great significance, representing the beginning of the next Cartwright generation.

Raising John in Albany during this era meant Joanna's days were likely filled with the daily tasks of childrearing, which demanded constant attention and skill. Infant mortality was high, so she would have been deeply attentive to his care and health, likely relying on a combination of folk remedies and the support of other women in the community. The community often shared collective childrearing knowledge, and it's likely that Joanna received advice from her own mother, Lydia, or other close family members and friends who'd experienced the joys and challenges of raising children in a frontier environment.

For Joanna and Richard, the birth of a son would have meant great hope for the future, especially in a society that placed importance on male heirs to carry on the family name, trade, and property. Though they were a relatively small colonial family, Albany's residents understood that building a lasting legacy in North America required strong family networks and resilient descendants. Richard would have begun considering what trade, skill, or education John would need to succeed. Though Albany was still a modest town, educational opportunities existed for those who could afford them, and even basic literacy and numeracy were highly valued skills.

As Albany was a Dutch-settled town transitioning into an increasingly English-speaking colony, Joanna would also have faced the decision of how to raise John in terms of language and culture. While the family likely spoke Dutch at home, especially given Joanna's own Dutch Reformed heritage, the town was becoming a blend of Dutch, English, and Indigenous influences. Joanna would have strived to balance the Cartwright family's future with the traditions she valued from her own upbringing, giving John an understanding of both his Dutch heritage and the wider colonial society in which he was being raised.

John's birth also coincided with a tense period as the colonies edged toward larger conflicts, with French and British powers competing for control over North America. Albany's position on the frontier meant that news of hostilities between these powers was common, and local families like the Cartwrights lived in a climate of watchful preparedness. Though little John wouldn't have known it, the threat of raids and battles—such as those that were already flaring up in King George's War (1744–1748)—meant his early years would be spent in a town on edge.

Still, everyday life in Albany persisted. For Joanna, family gatherings, church services, and seasonal festivals would have marked John's early years with a rhythm of community life and tradition. Church attendance would have been a cornerstone of John's childhood, with Sunday services, holidays, and baptisms creating a framework of faith around which the family's week revolved. As he grew, John would have been introduced to Dutch Reformed doctrines and the community values that defined colonial Albany, teaching him both respect for his heritage and resilience for the uncertain future.

Through John, Joanna found a renewed sense of purpose as she nurtured her young family, watching him grow into his role in Albany's community. His birth marked the continuation of the Cartwright name and an enduring legacy that Joanna hoped would flourish in the colonies for generations to come.

HERE'S A GENEALOGY travel itinerary based on Joanna Beasley's experience of welcoming her first child, John, in Albany, New York, in 1747:

**DAY 1: ARRIVAL AND Introduction to Colonial Albany**

Morning:

• Arrival in Albany, New York: Check into your accommodation. Recommended: Albany Hilton for its central location.

• Welcome Breakfast: Enjoy a traditional breakfast at the hotel and meet your genealogy guide.

Afternoon:

- Orientation Session: Visit the New York State Library to learn about the resources available for genealogical research, including family genealogies, local histories, and church records

Welcome To The Colonial Albany Project Website[60]

---

EVENING:

- Dinner: Dine at The Olde English Pub and Pantry, located in the historic Quackenbush Square

RESOURCE[61]

---

**DAY 2: EXPLORING DUTCH Heritage and Family Life**

Morning:

- First Church in Albany: Visit the oldest church in Albany, established in 1642, to understand its role in Joanna's family life and the community's religious practices

Sources on the People of Colonial Albany[62]

---

- CRAILO STATE HISTORIC Site: Explore this museum to learn about early Dutch settlers and see the interior of a traditional Dutch home.

Afternoon:

---

60. https://exhibitions.nysm.nysed.gov/albany/welcome.html

61. https://www.jstor.org/stable/23177373

62. https://exhibitions.nysm.nysed.gov/albany/sources.html

• Lunch: Enjoy a meal at Iron Gate Café, featuring recipes from the colonial era.

• Historical Walking Tour: Take a guided tour of Albany to see historical landmarks and learn about daily life in the 1740s

History of Albany, New York - Wikipedia[63]

EVENING:

• Lecture on Colonial Life: Attend a lecture on the social and cultural aspects of life in Albany during the mid-18th century

The Capital Moves to Albany: Editorial Note[64]

## DAY 3: RESEARCH AND Childrearing in Colonial Albany

Morning:

• Genealogical Research: Spend the morning at the New York State Archives in Albany, researching state records, including birth, marriage, and land records

Welcome To The Colonial Albany Project Website[65]

AFTERNOON:

• Albany Institute of History & Art: Visit this museum to explore exhibits on Albany's colonial history and art

---

63. https://en.wikipedia.org/wiki/History_of_Albany,_New_York

64. https://founders.archives.gov/documents/Jay/01-06-02-0257

65. https://exhibitions.nysm.nysed.gov/albany/welcome.html

The Albany Congress of 1754: Native People, Colonists & the Monarchy - New York Almanack[66]

---

• LUNCH: HAVE LUNCH at Jack's Oyster House, a historic Albany restaurant.

Evening:

• Community Gathering: Join a local community gathering to share stories and learn about the social fabric of colonial life.

---

## DAY 4: HISTORICAL CONTEXT and Personal Reflection

**Morning:**

• Hudson River Trade and Diplomacy: Visit sites along the Hudson River to understand its role in trade and diplomacy between English settlers, Dutch residents, and Indigenous nations

Albany's Role In Three Little-Remembered Colonial Wars in the Northeast - New York Almanack[67]

---

• FORT ORANGE: EXPLORE the site of the original Dutch settlement and learn about its significance in Albany's history

King George's War - Wikipedia[68]

---

66. https://www.newyorkalmanack.com/2022/01/the-albany-congress-of-1754-native-people-colonists-the-monarchy/

67. https://www.newyorkalmanack.com/2022/01/albany-colonial-wars-in-northeast/

68. https://en.wikipedia.org/wiki/King_George%27s_War

---

AFTERNOON:

• Lunch: Enjoy a meal at The Hollow Bar + Kitchen.

Welcome To The Colonial Albany Project Website[69]

RESOURCE[70]

---

• INTERACTIVE HISTORY Session: Participate in a reenactment or interactive session about life during the mid-18th century and the cultural exchanges in Albany

Seven Years War[71]

---

EVENING:

• Reflection and Discussion: Reflect on the day's experiences and discuss the impact of cultural exchanges on Joanna's life over dinner at Wellington's in the Renaissance Albany Hotel

The American Revolution Comes to Albany, New York, 1756-1776[72]

---

## DAY 5: DEPARTURE AND Final Research

Morning:

---

69. https://exhibitions.nysm.nysed.gov/albany/welcome.html

70. https://www.jstor.org/stable/23177373

71. https://exhibitions.nysm.nysed.gov/albany/7yw.html

72. https://allthingsliberty.com/2014/08/the-american-revolution-comes-to-albany-new-york-1756-1776/

- Final Research Session: Return to the New York State Library or Archives for any last-minute research.

- Farewell Brunch: Have a farewell brunch with your group at Wellington's in the Renaissance Albany Hotel.

Afternoon:

- Departure: Check out of your hotel and depart Albany with a deeper understanding of your family's history and the colonial era.

------

FEEL FREE TO ADJUST the itinerary based on your interests and research needs. Enjoy your genealogical journey in Albany!

------

AT THE AGE OF 22, JUST a year after the birth of her son John, Joanna gave birth to her second child, a daughter named Susannah, in 1748. Susannah's arrival added to the joy and responsibilities of Joanna's growing family. In the years that followed, Joanna's role as a mother expanded to include raising both a young son and now a daughter, which would have required even more of her attention, patience, and skill.

In colonial Albany, the birth of a daughter like Susannah would have been celebrated, though perhaps with less focus on inheritance and legacy compared to the birth of a son. However, as was common at the time, a daughter's upbringing was just as important in strengthening family ties and supporting the household. Joanna would have raised Susannah alongside John, ensuring she learned the skills needed to manage a home and perhaps even preparing her to eventually marry into another local family, thereby continuing the cycle of building alliances and networks.

Life in Albany for Joanna, Richard, and their children was still shaped by the rhythms of a colonial frontier town. While Joanna focused on her children, she also continued to manage the household and assist Richard in his business, likely contributing to the day-to-day management of any trade, farming, or community interactions he was involved in. Given Albany's proximity to both Native American groups and major trade routes, Richard might have had commercial dealings with Indigenous traders or other colonies, and Joanna's role as a homemaker could have included providing hospitality or managing correspondence related to his business.

As the years passed, Susanna would have witnessed the changing landscape of colonial life. With the ongoing tensions between French and British settlers, Albany's position on the frontier meant the family remained vulnerable to war or raids, although this would not have been a constant concern for a child. The community was generally protective, and both Joanna and Richard would have taken steps to ensure their children's safety and wellbeing. Like most young girls of the time, Susanna would have been taught domestic tasks such as cooking, sewing, and caring for younger siblings, learning from Joanna and other women in the community how to manage the household and contribute to family life.

Religious life continued to be central in the Cartwright household, with Joanna likely ensuring her children were raised in the Dutch Reformed faith, attending church services, and perhaps even participating in Bible readings at home. The religious revival sweeping through the colonies during this period, including the influence of the Great Awakening, would have also begun to make its way into Albany by the time Susanna was old enough to understand it. While Joanna's faith was firmly grounded in the Dutch Reformed tradition, the broader evangelical movements of the time may have introduced new ideas and sparked curiosity among her children about faith and personal spirituality.

As Susanna grew, her role in the family would have become more defined, especially in terms of assisting with household tasks and learning how to be a good wife and mother in her own right. By the time Susanna reached adolescence, she would have been expected to help Joanna care for John and any younger siblings, maintain the household, and perhaps start learning about the social intricacies of courting and marriage within the community.

Through these early years of raising both a son and a daughter, Joanna would have likely faced both the joys and challenges that came with motherhood—joy in seeing her children grow, learn, and become part of the wider community, but also the challenges of navigating the uncertain world of 18th-century colonial life. In Albany, with its blend of Dutch and English influences, and amidst the backdrop of rising tensions between the British and the French, Joanna's life as a mother in a growing family was still rooted in the traditions of her youth, yet marked by the ongoing changes and challenges of colonial life.

AT 24 YEARS OLD, JOANNA gave birth to her third child, a daughter named Elizabeth, on May 13, 1750, in Parish, New York. With the birth of Elizabeth, Joanna's responsibilities as a mother grew, and her family continued to expand, bringing with it a mix of joy and the challenges of raising a growing household. Elizabeth's arrival in Parish, a few years after Susanna, would have added to Joanna's already full life, and the two younger sisters would have likely grown up together, sharing their early years in the same environment of colonial New York.

In the 1750s, the colonial world was a place of both opportunity and uncertainty. The rivalry between the British and the French was intensifying, and the outbreak of the French and Indian War (1754–1763) would soon shape the lives of everyone in the region. For a young family like Joanna's, this conflict created a backdrop of tension and unease. Albany, being a key military and trade hub, would have been under the watchful eye of both settlers and soldiers, and the threat of war loomed large. Richard and Joanna, like other parents, would have tried to shield their children from the worst of these fears, but the risks of raids, skirmishes, and the potential for violence were never far from their thoughts.

However, in their everyday life, Joanna continued to focus on family and home, as any mother would. With three children now, Joanna's days would have been spent overseeing the care and upbringing of each, and Elizabeth, being the youngest at the time, would have received the bulk of her nurturing attention. Like her siblings, Elizabeth would have been raised with the expectations of a colonial child—learning the ways of the household, from domestic tasks such as sewing, cooking, and tending to animals, to the basics of managing a home.

The arrival of Elizabeth would also have meant more household work for Joanna. At this time, many families, especially those in rural New York, depended heavily on women to keep the household running. Joanna would have likely found support from other women in the community, perhaps her mother Lydia, other family members, or trusted neighbors. They would have shared resources, advice, and assistance when needed, especially when a new baby arrived. Elizabeth's older siblings, John and Susanna, would have pitched in by helping Joanna care for her and assist with household chores, a common practice in colonial families.

Church and community life continued to be central to Joanna's family, especially in these early years. The Dutch Reformed faith remained an important aspect of their daily routine, with regular attendance at church services and Christian teachings woven into the fabric of their lives. Elizabeth would have been raised in this environment, learning not only domestic skills but also how to be an active participant in the religious and social aspects of her community. The tight-knit religious community in Albany, with its sense of belonging and purpose, would have provided a strong foundation for Joanna's children, as they were taught to value their faith and community ties.

With Elizabeth's birth, Joanna would have also had to make important decisions regarding her children's future. For her daughters, especially as they approached adolescence, the focus would have turned to their future roles as wives and mothers. The social fabric of colonial life was built on marriage alliances, and both Joanna and Richard would have had to consider potential suitors for their daughters as they grew older.

Life in a colonial town like Albany was built on a sense of resilience and the constant balancing of duties. As Joanna raised her three children—John, Susanna, and Elizabeth—she navigated the complexities of frontier life, including the threat of war, the expectations of society, and the nurturing of her family. Each new addition to the family deepened the bonds within the household, even as the wider world around them became more uncertain.

Through the birth of Elizabeth, Joanna not only continued her role as a mother but also contributed to the larger tapestry of colonial New York. Each child represented hope for the future, the continuation of family and faith, and the ongoing challenge of raising children in a world full of both promise and peril. Joanna's life, like many of her contemporaries, was a constant cycle of nurturing her children, managing the household, and ensuring the legacy of her family endured in the ever-changing colonial landscape.

———

HERE'S A GENEALOGY travel itinerary based on Joanna's life in Parish, New York, during the 1750s:

———

## DAY 1: ARRIVAL AND Introduction to Colonial Life

Morning:

• Arrival in Parish, New York: Check into your accommodation. Recommended: Parish Bed & Breakfast for a cozy, historical stay.

• Welcome Breakfast: Enjoy a traditional breakfast at the B&B and meet your genealogy guide.

Afternoon:

• Orientation Session: Visit the Parish Historical Society to learn about the town's colonial history and resources available for genealogical research.

Evening:

• Dinner: Dine at The Parish Tavern, a local favorite with a colonial-inspired menu.

———

## DAY 2: EXPLORING DUTCH Heritage and Daily Life

Morning:

• Dutch Reformed Church: Visit the local Dutch Reformed Church to understand its influence on Joanna's family and community life

<u>Reformed Dutch and German churches of Manhattan and the Bronx | New York Genealogical & Biographical Society</u>[73]

------

• HISTORICAL WALKING Tour: Take a guided tour of Parish to see historical landmarks and learn about daily life in the 1750s.

Afternoon:

• Lunch: Enjoy a meal at Colonial Café, featuring recipes from the colonial era.

• Hands-On Workshop: Participate in a workshop on colonial domestic skills such as sewing, cooking, and animal care, reflecting Joanna's daily responsibilities.

Evening:

• Hudson River Influence: Attend a lecture on the Hudson River's role in trade and settlement during the colonial period.

------

## DAY 3: RESEARCH AND Community Connections

Morning:

• Genealogical Research: Spend the morning at the New York State Archives in Albany, researching state records, including birth, marriage, and land records

------

73. https://www.newyorkfamilyhistory.org/blog/reformed-dutch-and-german-churches-manhattan-and-bronx

<u>Quick tip: US Dutch Reformed Church Records Online</u>[74]

---

AFTERNOON:

• Albany Institute of History & Art: Visit this museum to explore exhibits on Albany's colonial history and art

<u>Religious Pluralism in the Middle Colonies, Divining America, TeacherServe®, National Humanities Center</u>[75]

---

• LUNCH: HAVE LUNCH at Jack's Oyster House, a historic Albany restaurant.

Evening:

• Community Gathering: Join a local community gathering to share stories and learn about the social fabric of colonial life.

---

## DAY 4: HISTORICAL CONTEXT and War Impact

Morning:

• French and Indian War Sites: Visit historical sites related to the French and Indian War to understand its impact on Joanna's family and the region

<u>RESOURCE</u>[76]

---

74. https://www.dutchgenealogy.nl/us-dutch-reformed-church-records-online/

75. https://nationalhumanitiescenter.org/tserve/eighteen/ekeyinfo/midcol.htm

76. https://academic.oup.com/cornell-scholarship-online/book/42268/chapter/356425331

• FORT TICONDEROGA: Explore this significant military site and learn about its role during the war

History of the RCA | Reformed Church in America[77]

AFTERNOON:

• Lunch: Enjoy a picnic at the fort with period-appropriate foods.

• Interactive History Session: Participate in a reenactment or interactive session about life during the French and Indian War.

Evening:

• Reflection and Discussion: Reflect on the day's experiences and discuss the war's impact on colonial families over dinner at The Hollow Bar + Kitchen.

## DAY 5: DEPARTURE AND Final Research

Morning:

• Final Research Session: Return to the New York State Library or Archives for any last-minute research.

• Farewell Brunch: Have a farewell brunch with your group at Wellington's in the Renaissance Albany Hotel.

Afternoon:

• Departure: Check out of your hotel and depart Parish with a deeper understanding of your family's history and the colonial era.

---

77. https://www.rca.org/about/history/

FEEL FREE TO ADJUST the itinerary based on your interests and research needs. Enjoy your genealogical journey in Parish and Albany!

AT THE AGE OF 26, JOANNA experienced the loss of her mother, Lydia Dally, who passed away in Albany in 1753. Lydia's death marked a significant turning point in Joanna's life, as the loss of a mother during this period often carried deep emotional and practical consequences. For Joanna, this would have meant the loss of not only a beloved parent but also a trusted advisor and a crucial source of support in both the emotional and day-to-day management of her household.

Lydia had likely been an important presence in Joanna's life, especially with the responsibilities of raising three young children. As was common at the time, family networks were key to surviving the difficult and often isolating nature of colonial life, and Joanna would have relied on her mother for assistance with childcare, advice on managing household affairs, and emotional support in the face of challenges. In the years leading up to Lydia's death, Joanna might have had her mother nearby to help care for the children, particularly the younger ones, while Joanna and Richard focused on the family's affairs.

Lydia's passing would have left Joanna with a sense of responsibility to her own children, but also a new void in her life. Joanna was now the matriarch of her own family and would have to take on a larger role in leading her household without the support of her mother. This would have been a difficult transition, as Joanna would have had to juggle the care of her children with the upkeep of the home and possibly the growing demands of Richard's business or any other commitments they had in Albany's community. In a society where extended family was integral to daily life, Joanna would have felt the absence of her mother deeply, both emotionally and in terms of practical support.

In terms of the community, Lydia's death would have had an impact on Joanna's social standing as well. In 18th-century colonial society, the death of a mother could shift the dynamics of familial obligations, and Joanna might have had to take on more responsibilities in the local church, as women in her position were often expected to assist in religious gatherings, provide for the poor, and manage charitable efforts. Her standing in the community, especially within the Dutch Reformed Church, would have likely increased as Joanna became a stronger presence in her own right.

For Joanna, this period of loss may have also caused her to reflect on her own place in the larger web of life. The thought of her children eventually becoming adults and facing their own challenges might have weighed heavily on her heart, knowing that she could not rely on her mother's wisdom and guidance for much longer. Joanna's grief would have been shared by her siblings, if she had any, and other members of her extended family. At the same time, Joanna would have had to stay focused on the needs of her own growing family, which would likely provide both comfort and distraction from the sadness of losing her mother.

Richard, too, would have had to support Joanna through this loss, though the emotional toll on him might have been different. As a husband, he would have had to step in as a partner in managing the household and helping with the children, but he might also have had his own responsibilities in the public sphere, possibly related to trade or other commitments. The death of Lydia could have drawn Richard and Joanna closer, as they navigated grief and responsibility together.

For Joanna's children, particularly John, Susanna, and Elizabeth, Lydia's passing would have meant the loss of a grandmother—a figure who had likely played an important role in their upbringing. In colonial times, extended families were often very close-knit, and Joanna's children might have been affected by their grandmother's death, even if they were still young.

Lydia's death, while marking a sorrowful moment in Joanna's life, also began to shift Joanna's role as she became the elder matriarch of her family. She would have to summon her own inner strength to carry on, both in the emotional sense and in her practical responsibilities as a wife, mother, and active member of the Albany community. This period of loss, while difficult, also marked a time when Joanna began to take on a larger role in shaping the future of her family and ensuring the continuation of their place in the colonial world.

---

HERE'S A GENEALOGY travel itinerary based on Joanna's life and the significant event of her mother Lydia's passing in Albany in 1753:

---

## DAY 1: ARRIVAL AND Introduction to Colonial Albany

Morning:

• Arrival in Albany, New York: Check into your accommodation. Recommended: Albany Hilton for its central location.

• Welcome Breakfast: Enjoy a traditional breakfast at the hotel and meet your genealogy guide.

Afternoon:

• Orientation Session: Visit the New York State Library to learn about the resources available for genealogical research, including family genealogies, local histories, and church records

<u>Genealogy Research in Albany Trip | NYG&B</u>[78]

---

EVENING:

• Dinner: Dine at The Olde English Pub and Pantry, located in the historic Quackenbush Square

<u>Research in Albany (Spring) | New York Genealogical & Biographical Society</u>[79]

---

## DAY 2: EXPLORING FAMILY and Community Life

Morning:

• Dutch Reformed Church: Visit the local Dutch Reformed Church to understand its influence on Joanna's family and community life

<u>3 Road Trip Itineraries for Albany County, New York</u>[80]

---

• HISTORICAL WALKING Tour: Take a guided tour of Albany to see historical landmarks and learn about daily life in the 1750s

<u>Itinerary Albany: Your Quick Guide to Exploring the City</u>[81]

---

AFTERNOON:

78. https://www.newyorkfamilyhistory.org/events/albany-genealogy-research-trip

79. https://www.newyorkfamilyhistory.org/events/research-albany-spring

80. https://www.albany.org/blog/post/road-trip-itineraries-for-albany-county/

81. https://familydestinationsguide.com/itinerary-albany/

• Lunch: Enjoy a meal at Iron Gate Café, featuring recipes from the colonial era.

• Hands-On Workshop: Participate in a workshop on colonial domestic skills such as sewing, cooking, and managing household affairs, reflecting Joanna's daily responsibilities.

Evening:

• Lecture on Colonial Life: Attend a lecture on the social and cultural aspects of life in Albany during the 1750s

Sources on the People of Colonial Albany[82]

---

## DAY 3: RESEARCH AND Reflection

Morning:

• Genealogical Research: Spend the morning at the New York State Archives in Albany, researching state records, including birth, marriage, and land records

Genealogy Research in Albany Trip | NYG&B[83]

---

AFTERNOON:

• Albany Institute of History & Art: Visit this museum to explore exhibits on Albany's colonial history and art

A Frontier Place: The Transformation of Colonial Albany, 1756-1763 - New York Almanack[84]

---

82. https://exhibitions.nysm.nysed.gov/albany/sources.html

83. https://www.newyorkfamilyhistory.org/events/albany-genealogy-research-trip

———————————

• LUNCH: HAVE LUNCH at Jack's Oyster House, a historic Albany restaurant.

Evening:

• Community Gathering: Join a local community gathering to share stories and learn about the social fabric of colonial life

Founding and History of the New York Colony[85]

———————————

## DAY 4: HISTORICAL CONTEXT and Personal Reflection

Morning:

• Visit to Lydia's Gravesite: Pay respects at the cemetery where Lydia Dally is buried, reflecting on her impact on Joanna's life and family

Early Albany Timeline[86]

Genealogy Research in Albany Trip | NYG&B[87]

Research in Albany (Spring) | New York Genealogical & Biographical Society[88]

———————————

84. https://www.newyorkalmanack.com/2022/12/a-frontier-place-the-transformation-of-colonial-albany-1756-1763/

85. https://www.thoughtco.com/new-york-colony-103878

86. https://exhibitions.nysm.nysed.gov/albany/timeline.html

87. https://www.newyorkfamilyhistory.org/events/albany-genealogy-research-trip

88. https://www.newyorkfamilyhistory.org/events/research-albany-spring

• TEN BROECK MANSION: Tour this historic home and learn about the Ten Broeck family and Albany's early history

Reformed Dutch and German churches of Manhattan and the Bronx | New York Genealogical & Biographical Society[89]

---

AFTERNOON:

• Lunch: Enjoy a meal at The Hollow Bar + Kitchen.

• Interactive History Session: Participate in a reenactment or interactive session about life during the 1750s and the impact of the French and Indian War on Albany

Quick tip: US Dutch Reformed Church Records Online[90]

---

EVENING:

• Reflection and Discussion: Reflect on the day's experiences and discuss the impact of Lydia's death on Joanna's life over dinner at Wellington's in the Renaissance Albany Hotel

Religious Pluralism in the Middle Colonies, Divining America, TeacherServe®, National Humanities Center[91]

---

**DAY 5: DEPARTURE AND Final Research**

---

89. https://www.newyorkfamilyhistory.org/blog/reformed-dutch-and-german-churches-manhattan-and-bronx

90. https://www.dutchgenealogy.nl/us-dutch-reformed-church-records-online/

91. https://nationalhumanitiescenter.org/tserve/eighteen/ekeyinfo/midcol.htm

Morning:

• Final Research Session: Return to the New York State Library or Archives for any last-minute research.

• Farewell Brunch: Have a farewell brunch with your group at Wellington's in the Renaissance Albany Hotel.

Afternoon:

• Departure: Check out of your hotel and depart Albany with a deeper understanding of your family's history and the colonial era.

---

FEEL FREE TO ADJUST the itinerary based on your interests and research needs. Enjoy your genealogical journey in Albany!

---

AT THE AGE OF 27, JOANNA lived through the tumultuous years of the French and Indian War (1754–1763), which would have had a significant impact on her life and the world around her. This war, fought primarily between British and French forces with various Native American tribes allied to each side, was a pivotal moment in the history of North America. For Joanna, living in Albany, New York—a strategic military and trade hub during this period—the war would have been a constant, looming presence that shaped the daily experiences of her family and community.

Albany, as a key point on the frontier and a center of British activity, was not far from the military campaigns, and the war's effects would have been felt in the town in a variety of ways. While Joanna's immediate life might have been primarily focused on her growing family, the war's influence would have been undeniable. Richard, as a man of business and connections in the community, might have been drawn into the logistics of wartime needs, such as supplying goods or trade, or perhaps even supporting British military efforts in some capacity. This involvement could have altered Joanna's daily routine, as she might have had to manage the household while Richard focused on the changing demands of wartime.

The French and Indian War led to increased military presence in the region, bringing soldiers and new settlers, which would have affected life in Albany. This influx of soldiers could have been both a blessing and a curse for Joanna's family. On one hand, it might have meant greater security as the British sought to fortify their positions, especially in relation to potential French or Native American attacks. On the other hand, it could have brought tension, as the presence of military forces in the town may have caused disruptions and fears of raids. The constant threat of violence or conflict from both French troops and Native American allies would have added an undercurrent of anxiety to Joanna's everyday life.

For Joanna, raising three young children during the war years would have been a significant challenge. With the uncertainties of war, especially in a frontier town like Albany, she would have had to stay vigilant, ensuring her children's safety while continuing to manage the household. She might have heard rumors of battles, troop movements, or the threat of French and Native American raids. These concerns would have weighed on her, but as with many women of her time, Joanna would have found ways to protect and care for her children, doing what was necessary to ensure they were safe and cared for.

The war itself brought about many social changes as well. Many families, especially those in frontier communities, faced disruptions in their normal routines. Some of the men of the community, including husbands, brothers, and fathers, were called to serve in the war, leaving women like Joanna to manage their homes on their own or with the help of extended family or neighbors. Joanna, as a mother of young children, would have been left to run the household and provide for her family, relying on her own resourcefulness and the support of others in the community.

Additionally, Joanna would have felt the economic strain of the war. While Albany was an important center of trade, the disruption of regular trade routes and the redirection of resources for the war effort likely led to shortages and inflation. Joanna would have had to be strategic in managing her household's resources—growing food, bartering for goods, and ensuring the children had what they needed despite the potential scarcity of certain items. This was a time when self-sufficiency and resilience were key, and Joanna's role in the family would have been indispensable.

Though the war was devastating and would ultimately have far-reaching consequences for the balance of power in North America, Joanna would have also seen the effects of the changing world on her children. As her children grew up during this time, they would have been exposed to the realities of colonial life in wartime—hearing about battles, seeing soldiers march through Albany, and perhaps even witnessing the emotional toll the war had on their parents and community.

For Joanna, the years of the French and Indian War would have been a time of hardship, sacrifice, and survival. It was a time when motherhood, community, and resilience became even more essential. The challenges of war only strengthened her ability to protect her family and maintain stability in the face of uncertainty. Through these years, Joanna's character was undoubtedly shaped by the demands of both motherhood and the realities of living in a war-torn region, fortifying her with the resolve that would carry her through not only this conflict but others that would follow in the years to come.

HERE'S A GENEALOGY travel itinerary based on Joanna Beasley's experience during the French and Indian War in Albany, New York:

## DAY 1: ARRIVAL AND Introduction to Colonial Albany

Morning:

• Arrival in Albany, New York: Check into your accommodation. Recommended: Albany Hilton for its central location.

• Welcome Breakfast: Enjoy a traditional breakfast at the hotel and meet your genealogy guide.

Afternoon:

• Orientation Session: Visit the New York State Library to learn about the resources available for genealogical research, including family genealogies, local histories, and church records

The French and Indian War: A New York Perspective[92]

EVENING:

• Dinner: Dine at The Olde English Pub and Pantry, located in the historic Quackenbush Square

Albany Plan of Union 1754 | American Battlefield Trust[93]

---

92. https://www.newyorkalmanack.com/2023/08/french-and-indian-war/

93. https://www.battlefields.org/learn/primary-sources/albany-plan-union-1754

## DAY 2: EXPLORING MILITARY and Trade History

Morning:

• Fort Orange: Explore the site of the original Dutch settlement and learn about its significance in Albany's history

RESOURCE[94]

---

• ALBANY INSTITUTE of History & Art: Visit this museum to explore exhibits on Albany's colonial history and art

A Frontier Place: The Transformation of Colonial Albany, 1756-1763 - New York Almanack[95]

---

AFTERNOON:

• Lunch: Enjoy a meal at Iron Gate Café, featuring recipes from the colonial era.

• Hudson River Trade and Diplomacy: Visit sites along the Hudson River to understand its role in trade and diplomacy between English settlers, Dutch residents, and Indigenous nations

The American Revolution Comes to Albany, New York, 1756-1776[96]

---

94. https://bing.com/

search?q=French+and+Indian+War+impact+on+Albany+New+York&form=SKPBOT

95. https://www.newyorkalmanack.com/2022/12/a-frontier-place-the-transformation-of-colonial-albany-1756-1763/

96. https://allthingsliberty.com/2014/08/the-american-revolution-comes-to-albany-new-york-1756-1776/

EVENING:

• Lecture on Colonial Life: Attend a lecture on the social and cultural aspects of life in Albany during the mid-18th century

Schenectady massacre - Wikipedia[97]

---

## DAY 3: RESEARCH AND Family Life During Wartime

Morning:

• Genealogical Research: Spend the morning at the New York State Archives in Albany, researching state records, including birth, marriage, and land records

The French and Indian War: A New York Perspective[98]

---

AFTERNOON:

• First Church in Albany: Visit the oldest church in Albany, established in 1642, to understand its role in Joanna's family life and the community's religious practices.

• Lunch: Have lunch at Jack's Oyster House, a historic Albany restaurant.

Evening:

• Community Gathering: Join a local community gathering to share stories and learn about the social fabric of colonial life

RESOURCE[99]

97. https://en.wikipedia.org/wiki/Schenectady_massacre

98. https://www.newyorkalmanack.com/2023/08/french-and-indian-war/

## DAY 4: HISTORICAL CONTEXT and Personal Reflection

Morning:

• Military Presence in Albany: Visit sites that highlight the British military presence in Albany during the French and Indian War

Seven Years War[100]

• SCHENECTADY COUNTY Historical Society: Explore exhibits on the impact of the French and Indian War on local communities

Discover the History of Albany, New York[101]

AFTERNOON:

The French and Indian War: A New York Perspective[102]

Albany Plan of Union 1754 | American Battlefield Trust[103]

LUNCH: ENJOY A MEAL at The Hollow Bar + Kitchen.

• Interactive History Session: Participate in a reenactment or interactive session about life during the mid-18th century and the cultural exchanges in Albany

99. https://www.jstor.org/stable/23177373

100. https://exhibitions.nysm.nysed.gov/albany/7yw.html

101. https://www.albany.com/about-albany/history/

102. https://www.newyorkalmanack.com/2023/08/french-and-indian-war/

103. https://www.battlefields.org/learn/primary-sources/albany-plan-union-1754

History of Albany, NY[104]

---

EVENING:

• Reflection and Discussion: Reflect on the day's experiences and discuss the impact of cultural exchanges on Joanna's life over dinner at Wellington's in the Renaissance Albany Hotel

City History | Albany, NY[105]

---

## DAY 5: DEPARTURE AND Final Research

Morning:

• Final Research Session: Return to the New York State Library or Archives for any last-minute research.

• Farewell Brunch: Have a farewell brunch with your group at Wellington's in the Renaissance Albany Hotel.

Afternoon:

• Departure: Check out of your hotel and depart Albany with a deeper understanding of your family's history and the colonial era.

---

FEEL FREE TO ADJUST the itinerary based on your interests and research needs. Enjoy your genealogical journey in Albany!

---

104. https://www.albany.org/things-to-do/albany-heritage-tourism/history/

105. http://albanyny.gov/512/City-History

AT THE AGE OF 28, JOANNA'S life saw another significant event—the birth of her daughter, Catherine, on March 10, 1754, in New York City. Joanna had now become a mother of four, with a growing family to care for in the midst of the ongoing French and Indian War. The birth of a child during this time would have been both a joyous and challenging event, as Joanna balanced the demands of raising young children with the turbulent circumstances of the war.

New York City, as one of the most important and bustling urban centers in the colonies, would have been a much different environment than the smaller, more rural Albany. The city was a key point of trade, culture, and politics, and Joanna's decision to give birth there suggests a significant shift in her life circumstances, perhaps related to Richard's work or the desire for better healthcare during childbirth. The presence of a large population and the bustling commercial activity in New York City would have exposed Joanna to a diverse array of people, goods, and services, but it also meant that she faced the challenges of living in a busy, potentially less secure urban environment during the war.

Joanna's fourth child, Catherine, was likely born into a time of great uncertainty. While her other children were growing up in Albany, Catherine's early years would have been shaped by the dynamic, rapidly changing environment of New York City during a period of war. The city itself was a central hub for the British military, and its proximity to conflict zones meant that it could be subject to the ebb and flow of war-related activity. The British military maintained a strong presence there, and Joanna would have likely felt the tension of living so close to military operations. As a mother, Joanna would have been concerned with keeping her family safe in the midst of a city that could be affected by both British troop movements and the ever-present threat of attacks from the French or their Native American allies.

In terms of daily life, Joanna would have relied on a network of women—friends, family, and midwives—to help with the birth and the early care of Catherine. While the city offered more medical resources than a frontier town like Albany, the realities of 18th-century childbirth meant that Joanna's experience was still one that involved considerable risk. Given the demands of motherhood and household management, Joanna would have worked hard to ensure that her family continued to thrive despite the hardships of war and living in an urban environment.

Catherine's birth marked another milestone in Joanna's life, as the arrival of a new child added to her responsibilities and the weight of raising a family during wartime. Joanna, having already experienced the birth and growth of three other children, would have been well-versed in the challenges of motherhood. However, each birth brings its own set of circumstances, and Catherine's arrival was likely greeted with a mixture of joy, relief, and exhaustion, as Joanna navigated the physical and emotional demands of caring for a newborn while managing the older children and household responsibilities.

Given the broader context of the time, Joanna's children—including Catherine—were likely exposed to the sounds of soldiers marching, the hum of war-related activities, and the discussions of adults about the course of the war. Joanna may have shielded her younger children from the more difficult aspects of wartime life, but they would have been aware of the ongoing conflict and the dangers it posed. The birth of Catherine, though a moment of personal happiness for Joanna, was also another layer of complexity in a world that was increasingly affected by the war.

As Joanna entered her late 20s and early 30s, the pressures on her family continued to mount. Raising young children during this period, while also facing the emotional and physical toll of the French and

Indian War, would have been overwhelming. Joanna's ability to keep her family intact, to ensure their survival and well-being, would have been a testament to her strength and resilience. Catherine's birth was one more chapter in the story of Joanna's motherhood, marked by both personal growth and the continual challenges of raising children in a world at war.

―――――

HERE'S A GENEALOGY travel itinerary based on Joanna Beasley's experience of giving birth to her daughter, Catherine, in New York City during the French and Indian War:

―――――

## DAY 1: ARRIVAL AND Introduction to Colonial New York City

Morning:

• Arrival in New York City: Check into your accommodation. Recommended: The Beekman, A Thompson Hotel for its historic charm.

• Welcome Breakfast: Enjoy a traditional breakfast at the hotel and meet your genealogy guide.

Afternoon:

• Orientation Session: Visit the New York Public Library to learn about the resources available for genealogical research, including family genealogies, local histories, and church records.

Evening:

• Dinner: Dine at Fraunces Tavern, a historic site that dates back to the colonial era

History of New York City - Wikipedia[106]

---

## DAY 2: EXPLORING COLONIAL Life and Military Presence

Morning:

• Trinity Church: Visit this historic church, established in 1697, to understand its role in Joanna's family life and the community's religious practices

Set Your Time Machine for 1754 | The New York Society Library[107]

---

• NEW-YORK HISTORICAL Society: Explore exhibits on New York City's colonial history and the impact of the French and Indian War.

Afternoon:

• Lunch: Enjoy a meal at The Odeon, a restaurant with a vintage New York vibe.

• British Military Presence: Visit sites that highlight the British military presence in New York City during the French and Indian War

The History of Midwifery and Childbirth in America: A Time Line[108]

---

EVENING:

---

106. https://en.wikipedia.org/wiki/History_of_New_York_City

107. https://www.nysoclib.org/blog/set-your-time-machine-1754

108. https://www.midwiferytoday.com/web-article/history-midwifery-childbirth-america-time-line/

• Lecture on Colonial Life: Attend a lecture on the social and cultural aspects of life in New York City during the mid-18th century

Changes in childbirth in the United States: 1750–1950 - Hektoen International[109]

---

## DAY 3: RESEARCH AND Family Life During Wartime

Morning:

• Genealogical Research: Spend the morning at the New York Genealogical and Biographical Society, researching state records, including birth, marriage, and land records.

Afternoon:

• Midwifery and Childbirth in the 18th Century: Visit the Museum of the City of New York to learn about the history of midwifery and childbirth during Joanna's time

What is the History of Midwifery?[110]

---

• LUNCH: HAVE LUNCH at Katz's Delicatessen, a historic New York eatery.

Evening:

• Community Gathering: Join a local community gathering to share stories and learn about the social fabric of colonial life

History of Childbirth in America[111]

---

109. https://hekint.org/2017/01/27/changes-in-childbirth-in-the-united-states-1750-1950/

110. https://www.registerednursing.org/articles/history-midwifery/

---

## DAY 4: HISTORICAL CONTEXT and Personal Reflection

Morning:

• Hudson River Trade and Diplomacy: Visit sites along the Hudson River to understand its role in trade and diplomacy between English settlers, Dutch residents, and Indigenous nations

The French and Indian War (1754-1763): Its Consequences | American Battlefield Trust[112]

---

• FRAUNCES TAVERN MUSEUM: Explore this museum to learn about its significance in New York City's history

History of New York City - Wikipedia[113]

---

AFTERNOON:

• Lunch: Enjoy a meal at The Dutch, a restaurant inspired by New York's diverse culinary history.

History of New York City - Wikipedia[114]

Set Your Time Machine for 1754 | The New York Society Library[115]

---

111. https://www.jstor.org/stable/3173968

112. https://www.battlefields.org/learn/articles/french-and-indian-war-1754-1763-its-consequences

113. https://en.wikipedia.org/wiki/History_of_New_York_City

114. https://en.wikipedia.org/wiki/History_of_New_York_City

115. https://www.nysoclib.org/blog/set-your-time-machine-1754

• INTERACTIVE HISTORY Session: Participate in a reenactment or interactive session about life during the mid-18th century and the cultural exchanges in New York City

<u>French and Indian War - Seven Years War | HISTORY</u>[116]

---

EVENING:

• Reflection and Discussion: Reflect on the day's experiences and discuss the impact of cultural exchanges on Joanna's life over dinner at The Beekman Hotel's Temple Court Restaurant

<u>New York Colony Facts</u>[117]

---

116. https://www.history.com/topics/native-american-history/french-and-indian-war

117. https://www.americanhistorycentral.com/entries/new-york-colony/

Morning:

• Final Research Session: Return to the New York Public Library or Genealogical Society for any last-minute research.

• Farewell Brunch: Have a farewell brunch with your group at Temple Court Restaurant in The Beekman Hotel.

Afternoon:

• Departure: Check out of your hotel and depart New York City with a deeper understanding of your family's history and the colonial era.

---

FEEL FREE TO ADJUST the itinerary based on your interests and research needs. Enjoy your genealogical journey in New York City!

---

SUSANNAH WAS BORN BEFORE September 4, 1757, in New York Colony. She arrived in the world just before the French and Indian War truly intensified in the years that followed. A child born into this turbulent world, named in memory of her sister Susanna, could have carried a weight of meaning far beyond her years.

It was not uncommon in the 18th century for names to serve as symbols—vessels of memory and legacy—and Susannah's name would certainly have been a living tribute to the sibling she never knew. Her birth could very well have been seen as a continuation, a quiet defiance against the capriciousness of fate that had taken her sister Susanna away. The Cartwrights, no strangers to the hardships of colonial life, likely found in this act of naming both a means of remembrance and renewal.

Joanna, no doubt, would have held her new daughter in her arms with a mixture of joy and sorrow—a new life, yes, but one that carried the memory of the daughter who had been lost too soon. The hope of healing through Susannah's birth would have been palpable, her name a balm to the wounds left by Susanna's untimely departure. It was as though the family said, "We shall not let this memory fade; we will carry it forward."

The timing, too, adds layers of context. Born just before September 4, 1757, Susannah's arrival likely took place during a time when New York Colony was still feeling the tremors of earlier colonial skirmishes and the looming threat of further conflict. The world Joanna and Richard inhabited was one of uncertainty. Still, in naming their new daughter in honor of their first, they were, in their way, creating a small pocket of stability, of continuity, amidst the chaos.

And the naming itself—oh, how the Cartwrights must have amused themselves over the close resemblance between the names Susanna and Susannah! It is a playful yet poignant reminder of how names were often reused in families, as if the very sound of a name could somehow bring a lost soul back. Perhaps in their hearts, Joanna and Richard hoped that Susannah might carry the spirit of her sister, the one who had been taken too soon, into a future that might be kinder to her.

So, as Susannah grew up in the New York Colony, perhaps a little more adored, a little more cherished, she would have known that her name was a link to her sister's memory, and that, despite the hard times, the love that came with it was a legacy all its own.

***

AT THE AGE OF 29, JOANNA experienced the birth of a son named Henry, on December 7, 1755, in New York City. As a mother to a growing family, Joanna was now faced with the challenge of raising five children during an incredibly difficult period in colonial American history—the French and Indian War was still raging, and the uncertainties of war and political unrest continued to shape the lives of families like hers.

By the time Henry was born, the war had already been ongoing for more than a year, and the effects of the conflict were becoming more pronounced. New York City, being a major British stronghold, was a critical location during this time. British troops were stationed there, and the city was a hub for military strategy, logistics, and supply lines. For Joanna, living in a city so central to the war effort would have meant a constant awareness of the ongoing conflict and the tensions that accompanied it. The presence of soldiers, military activity, and the fear of potential French or Native American raids would have added an extra layer of stress to her daily life.

The birth of Henry, though a joyous occasion, would have been influenced by the challenging environment around her. Childbirth in 18th-century New York City still posed significant risks. While Joanna would have had access to more medical resources than in smaller towns, the practice of medicine at the time was still rudimentary. Complications during birth were common, and Joanna would have had to rely on midwives, family members, and possibly local doctors to help her through the process.

Managing the household with five children, all while living in an environment marked by uncertainty and war, would have been overwhelming for Joanna. The war meant that Richard—her husband—might have been more involved with military logistics or trade that supported the British army, leaving Joanna to manage the household on her own. While Richard's connections in the community could have provided some financial stability, the challenges of raising young children in a war-torn city would have placed great physical and emotional demands on Joanna.

New York City, as a bustling port city, was also dealing with the economic and social effects of the war. Supplies and goods that were essential for everyday life were increasingly diverted for military use, which meant that ordinary families like Joanna's might have faced shortages or inflation. Goods such as food, cloth, and other essentials were becoming harder to come by, and Joanna likely had to be resourceful in stretching her family's resources. The scarcity of goods and the rising prices, combined with the influx of soldiers and displaced families, would have created a tense atmosphere in the city. Joanna would have had to maintain a sense of normalcy in her household, providing food, care, and attention to her children, even while the world around her seemed to be in a constant state of flux.

The birth of Henry also brought more challenges in terms of security. The French and Indian War had an unpredictable nature, and even in the relative safety of New York City, the fear of potential attacks was ever-present. Joanna would have likely worried about the safety of her children, especially Henry, as the youngest of her sons. The sound of distant gunfire or the movement of troops would have served as constant reminders of the larger war effort.

Yet, in the midst of these hardships, the arrival of Henry was a moment of joy for Joanna and her family. She had already experienced the births of her other children and had developed resilience in raising them, but each child brought their own unique challenges. As Henry grew, Joanna would have watched him join his siblings in navigating the world shaped by war, scarcity, and change. The bond between mother and child, though tested by external pressures, would have only deepened as Joanna continued to care for her young family.

Joanna's life at the time was one of perseverance and adaptability. She was a mother not just to Henry, but to her other children, ensuring that each was nurtured and protected amid the chaos of their environment. While New York City was a major center of British power during the war, it was also a city exposed to the dangers and uncertainties of the ongoing conflict. Joanna's experiences during Henry's early years would have shaped the course of her motherhood, as she continued to provide a stable and loving home for her growing family, even as the world around her was anything but stable.

———

ON FEBRUARY 2, 1759, Joanna Beasley Cartwright and her husband Richard welcomed their son Richard into the world in Albany, New York. At the time, Joanna was 32 years old, and her family was growing, even as the world around them remained unsettled. The year 1759 was notable for being in the middle of the French and Indian War, a conflict that had a profound effect on the lives of colonists in New York and throughout the colonies.

As a mother of multiple children by now, Joanna had experience in raising a family, but the birth of Richard likely brought a new sense of hope and continuity. The Cartwrights were living in a time of great uncertainty, yet each new life in their family represented a promise of perseverance—a way to carry on despite the challenges of war and the unpredictable nature of colonial life.

Richard, the child, was named after his father, a common practice of the time that helped ensure the continuity of family names across generations. His birth would have been a joyous occasion for the family, even if tempered by the difficult realities of the period. The infant would have been born into a world shaped by the ongoing war, where family security was never guaranteed, and survival often depended on the ability to adapt and remain resilient.

Albany, in particular, had a strategic significance during this time as a military and trade hub, and it was likely a bustling, tense place as colonial forces prepared for battle and dealt with the fallout of ongoing conflicts with French and Native American forces. While the Cartwrights were not directly involved in the fighting, the war's effects on everyday life would have been hard to avoid. Families lived in constant anticipation of what the future held—whether they would face new threats, be forced to flee, or suffer further losses.

For Joanna, the birth of her son Richard may have been a bittersweet blessing—another child to raise, another source of love, yet another reminder of the fragility of life. Given the historical context, it is likely that Joanna and Richard would have been aware of the possibility of loss—infant mortality was common in this era, and the war posed additional risks to families. Still, Joanna's resilience would have been key to navigating these challenges. As a mother, she would have done all she could to protect her children, and Richard's arrival would have given her renewed strength and purpose, even as she continued to bear the weight of history's uncertainty.

<hr>

AT 36 YEARS OLD, JOANNA Beasley Cartwright faced the loss of her half-brother, Johannes Van Benthuysen, in 1763. Johannes's death marked another chapter of grief in Joanna's life, one that would be felt deeply within the family. The loss of a sibling, even a half-sibling, was never easy, especially in a time where death was a much more present part of daily life, whether due to the harsh conditions of colonial living or the ongoing conflicts like the French and Indian War.

Johannes, like Joanna, had been born into a world full of complexities, the son of Lydia Dally from her earlier relationship, and now, with his passing, Joanna would have been reminded of the intricate family ties that bound them all. While Johannes might not have been as central to

Joanna's life as her immediate family members, his death still marked a significant moment. It was a reminder that family, in all its forms—by blood or by circumstance—was fragile, and life was never certain.

In the years leading up to Johannes's death, Joanna had already experienced several heartaches: the loss of her daughter Susanna, the turbulence of the French and Indian War, and the responsibility of raising multiple children in a world filled with uncertainty. The passing of Johannes would have been another heavy moment in the cycle of life and death, particularly in a colonial society where death could come from disease, war, or other unforeseen circumstances.

The year 1763 also marked the end of the French and Indian War, and while the Treaty of Paris was signed that year, the impact of the war would still have been deeply felt by families like the Cartwrights. It is likely that Joanna, now a mother of several children, found herself reflecting on the fragility of life and the importance of the family she had built.

Joanna's strength, honed through years of hardship, would have been called upon once again. As a mother, a wife, and now a sister who had to mourn the loss of Johannes, Joanna would have drawn on all of her resilience to support those around her. It was a difficult period, but Joanna, despite her grief, would have continued to navigate the challenges of life, raising her children, and maintaining her role in her community.

Her half-brother's passing in 1763 may have also served as a reminder of the brevity of life during this turbulent time in colonial New York, and as Joanna moved forward, she would have carried this sorrow with her, even as she worked to protect and nurture the family she had left.

AT 38 YEARS OLD, JOANNA Beasley Cartwright lived through the rising tensions that gripped the American colonies in 1765. This was the year the British Parliament passed the Stamp Act, bypassing the colonial assemblies and imposing a series of internal and external taxes on the outraged colonists. The political landscape shifted dramatically, and Joanna, now a mother of several children and an experienced matriarch, would have felt the ripple effects of these changes in her community.

The imposition of these taxes—including the Stamp Act, which taxed paper goods and legal documents—was a direct challenge to the colonists' sense of autonomy. For Joanna and her family in New York, a colony that had both strong loyalist factions and a growing sense of colonial resistance, the economic and social impact would have been palpable. With the introduction of the Stamp Act, everyday items like newspapers, legal papers, and even playing cards were taxed, sparking widespread protest. The tax burden weighed heavily on the colonists, many of whom were already struggling with the aftermath of the French and Indian War.

Joanna, now living through a time of great political and social unrest, would have witnessed the shift in attitudes among her neighbors and friends. The political upheaval was personal, and as a mother, she would have been concerned about the future of her children in a society on the verge of open rebellion. The emotional and economic strain would have been felt deeply in a family already familiar with hardship—both from the perils of colonial life and the toll of previous wars and losses.

The British taxes, particularly the Stamp Act, angered many colonists and led to widespread protests. In New York, as in other colonies, the resistance to British rule began to coalesce, with groups like the Sons of Liberty organizing opposition to the new taxes. Joanna, who had lived through the challenges of early colonial life, would likely have witnessed the growing divide between loyalists and patriots in her community, perhaps even feeling the pressure to align with one side or the other, although her loyalty to her family and their survival may have been her primary concern.

As tensions mounted, Joanna would also have seen how the protests began to take shape—boycotts of British goods, street demonstrations, and public outcries against the perceived injustice of the Stamp Act. Her household, like many others, would have been caught up in the wider currents of change, as the growing unrest brought a heightened sense of awareness about colonial rights, self-governance, and independence.

At 38, Joanna was no stranger to the pressures of colonial life, but the mounting resistance to British rule would have been a new challenge—one that required a delicate balance of maintaining the well-being of her family while navigating the changing political environment. The Stamp Act was a precursor to even greater tensions, and Joanna, whose life had already been marked by loss and adversity, would have had to adapt once again, this time to a world where the very fabric of the colonies was beginning to unravel, setting the stage for the American Revolution.

***

AT 38 YEARS OLD, JOANNA Beasley Cartwright lived through the rising tensions that gripped the American colonies in 1765. This was the year the British Parliament passed the Stamp Act, bypassing the colonial assemblies and imposing a series of internal and external taxes on the outraged colonists. The political landscape shifted dramatically, and Joanna, now a mother of several children and an experienced matriarch, would have felt the ripple effects of these changes in her community.

The imposition of these taxes—including the Stamp Act, which taxed paper goods and legal documents—was a direct challenge to the colonists' sense of autonomy. For Joanna and her family in New York, a colony that had both strong loyalist factions and a growing sense of colonial resistance, the economic and social impact would have been palpable. With the introduction of the Stamp Act, everyday items like newspapers, legal papers, and even playing cards were taxed, sparking widespread protest. The tax burden weighed heavily on the colonists, many of whom were already struggling with the aftermath of the French and Indian War.

Joanna, now living through a time of great political and social unrest, would have witnessed the shift in attitudes among her neighbors and friends. The political upheaval was personal, and as a mother, she would have been concerned about the future of her children in a society on the verge of open rebellion. The emotional and economic strain would have been felt deeply in a family already familiar with hardship—both from the perils of colonial life and the toll of previous wars and losses.

The British taxes, particularly the Stamp Act, angered many colonists and led to widespread protests. In New York, as in other colonies, the resistance to British rule began to coalesce, with groups like the Sons of Liberty organizing opposition to the new taxes. Joanna, who had lived through the challenges of early colonial life, would likely have witnessed the growing divide between loyalists and patriots in her community, perhaps even feeling the pressure to align with one side or the other, although her loyalty to her family and their survival may have been her primary concern.

As tensions mounted, Joanna would also have seen how the protests began to take shape—boycotts of British goods, street demonstrations, and public outcries against the perceived injustice of the Stamp Act. Her household, like many others, would have been caught up in the wider currents of change, as the growing unrest brought a heightened sense of awareness about colonial rights, self-governance, and independence.

At 38, Joanna was no stranger to the pressures of colonial life, but the mounting resistance to British rule would have been a new challenge—one that required a delicate balance of maintaining the well-being of her family while navigating the changing political environment. The Stamp Act was a precursor to even greater tensions, and Joanna, whose life had already been marked by loss and adversity, would have had to adapt once again, this time to a world where the very fabric of the colonies was beginning to unravel, setting the stage for the American Revolution.

HERE'S A GENEALOGY travel itinerary based on Joanna Beasley Cartwright's experience during the rising tensions of 1765 in New York City:

**DAY 1: ARRIVAL AND Introduction to Colonial New York City**

Morning:

• Arrival in New York City: Check into your accommodation. Recommended: The Beekman, A Thompson Hotel for its historic charm.

• Welcome Breakfast: Enjoy a traditional breakfast at the hotel and meet your genealogy guide.

Afternoon:

• Orientation Session: Visit the New York Public Library to learn about the resources available for genealogical research, including family genealogies, local histories, and church records

Early settlers of New York State : their ancestors and descendants : Foley, Janet Wethy : Free Download, Borrow, and Streaming : Internet Archive[118]

EVENING:

• Dinner: Dine at Fraunces Tavern, a historic site that dates back to the colonial era

New York Colony Facts[119]

## DAY 2: EXPLORING COLONIAL Life and Political Unrest

Morning:

• Trinity Church: Visit this historic church, established in 1697, to understand its role in Joanna's family life and the community's religious practices

A Glimpse at Everyday Life in the New England Colonies, 1763-1774 | American Battlefield Trust[120]

---

118. https://archive.org/details/earlysettlersofn13fole

119. https://www.americanhistorycentral.com/entries/new-york-colony/

120. https://www.battlefields.org/learn/articles/glimpse-everyday-life-new-england-colonies-1763-1774

• NEW-YORK HISTORICAL Society: Explore exhibits on New York City's colonial history and the impact of the Stamp Act

RESOURCE[121]

---

AFTERNOON:

• Lunch: Enjoy a meal at The Odeon, a restaurant with a vintage New York vibe.

• British Military Presence: Visit sites that highlight the British military presence in New York City during the Stamp Act crisis

Life in Colonial America Prior to the Revolutionary War | American Battlefield Trust[122]

---

EVENING:

• Lecture on Colonial Life: Attend a lecture on the social and cultural aspects of life in New York City during the mid-18th century

Stamp Act - Fact, Reaction & Legacy | HISTORY[123]

---

DAY 3: RESEARCH AND Family Life During Political Unrest

Morning:

---

121. https://www.jstor.org/stable/2703309

122. https://www.battlefields.org/learn/articles/life-colonial-america-prior-revolutionary-war

123. https://www.history.com/topics/american-revolution/stamp-act

• Genealogical Research: Spend the morning at the New York Genealogical and Biographical Society, researching state records, including birth, marriage, and land records

Early settlers of New York State : their ancestors and descendants : Foley, Janet Wethy : Free Download, Borrow, and Streaming : Internet Archive[124]

---

AFTERNOON:

• Sons of Liberty and Protests: Visit sites associated with the Sons of Liberty and learn about their role in resisting the Stamp Act

Stamp Act Congress (1765) | U.S. History, Significance, & Definition | Britannica[125]

---

• LUNCH: HAVE LUNCH at Katz's Delicatessen, a historic New York eatery.

Evening:

• Community Gathering: Join a local community gathering to share stories and learn about the social fabric of colonial life

The Stamp Act in New York, 1765, Part I - Washington & Hamilton, Central Park, Brooklyn Walking Tours[126]

---

**DAY 4: HISTORICAL CONTEXT and Personal Reflection**

---

124. https://archive.org/details/earlysettlersofn13fole

125. https://www.britannica.com/topic/Stamp-Act-Congress

126. https://www.revolutionarytoursnyc.com/2021/06/01/the-stamp-act-in-new-york-1765-part-i/

Morning:

• Hudson River Trade and Diplomacy: Visit sites along the Hudson River to understand its role in trade and diplomacy between English settlers, Dutch residents, and Indigenous nations

"The Stamp Act: Revolutionary Resistance in New York" by Ryan L. Wagner[127]

RESOURCE[128]

New York Colony Facts[129]

---

• FRAUNCES TAVERN MUSEUM: Explore this museum to learn about its significance in New York City's history

New York Colony Facts[130]

---

AFTERNOON:

• Lunch: Enjoy a meal at The Dutch, a restaurant inspired by New York's diverse culinary history.

• Interactive History Session: Participate in a reenactment or interactive session about life during the mid-18th century and the cultural exchanges in New York City

Stamp Act, Summary, Significance, American Revolution, APUSH[131]

---


127. https://digitalcommons.buffalostate.edu/history_theses/44/

128. https://archive.org/details/earlysettlersofn13fole

129. https://www.americanhistorycentral.com/entries/new-york-colony/

130. https://www.americanhistorycentral.com/entries/new-york-colony/

131. https://www.americanhistorycentral.com/entries/stamp-act/

EVENING:

• Reflection and Discussion: Reflect on the day's experiences and discuss the impact of cultural exchanges on Joanna's life over dinner at The Beekman Hotel's Temple Court Restaurant

Sons of Liberty Explained | Who They Were & What They Did[132]

DAY 5: DEPARTURE AND Final Research

Morning:

• Final Research Session: Return to the New York Public Library or Genealogical Society for any last-minute research.

• Farewell Brunch: Have a farewell brunch with your group at Temple Court Restaurant in The Beekman Hotel.

Afternoon:

• Departure: Check out of your hotel and depart New York City with a deeper understanding of your family's history and the colonial era.

FEEL FREE TO ADJUST the itinerary based on your interests and research needs. Enjoy your genealogical journey in New York City!

AT 42 YEARS OLD, JOANNA Beasley Cartwright faced another personal loss when her father, John "James" Francis Beasley, passed away in Albany on August 15, 1768. This marked a significant moment

---

132. https://www.americanrevolution.org/sons-of-liberty/

in Joanna's life, as she had already endured the loss of her mother, Lydia Dally, and now the death of her father left her with no surviving parents.

Her father's death would have been a bittersweet moment, as Joanna likely reflected on the complexities of their relationship, shaped by her early life in Albany and the evolving family dynamics. As the daughter of John Beasley, a figure who had shaped her formative years, Joanna would have been deeply affected by his passing, particularly as she had now reached a point in life where she was a mother herself. The loss of a parent often brings a realization of one's own place in the family lineage, and Joanna would have felt the weight of her new role as the matriarch in her family.

By this time, Joanna was a seasoned woman who had lived through the challenges of colonial life, raising children in an era of conflict, loss, and social upheaval. The death of her father would have added to the emotional burden she already carried, especially as the political climate in the colonies grew more tense. The Stamp Act protests had given way to broader movements for independence, and by 1768, the seeds of revolution were being sown. As a woman living through such tumultuous times, Joanna's family, already familiar with loss, would have felt the effects of both personal and political upheavals.

Joanna's father had been part of her early life in Albany, and with his passing, Joanna would have had to take on even more responsibility in the community. At the same time, the mourning of a father would have allowed her to reflect on the passage of time and the legacy of the Beasley family. Though Joanna had already lived through much, including the challenges of raising children, maintaining her marriage to Richard Cartwright, and dealing with the pressures of colonial life, the death of her father would have marked another turning point—her full transition into the role of the elder generation.

In a society that still placed much weight on familial ties, Joanna's loss would have been felt deeply not only within her immediate family but also within the broader Albany community, where family names carried weight. It's possible Joanna would have found herself more deeply embedded in the local support networks, as she navigated the complexities of being a wife, mother, and now the oldest living member of her immediate family.

While Joanna's father had passed, her legacy as a matriarch of the Cartwright family and the community would continue to grow. The grief she experienced would have shaped her outlook, but so would the resilience that had defined her life up to this point. The years ahead would be marked by continued challenges and political unrest, but Joanna's ability to navigate loss and adversity would have served her well as she entered the next chapter of her life.

AS A LOYALIST DURING the American Revolution, Joanna Beasley Cartwright, alongside her husband Richard Cartwright, found themselves on the opposing side of the colonial rebels. Their loyalty to the British Crown would have placed them in an increasingly precarious position as tensions between the colonists and Britain escalated throughout the 1770s.

By the time of the Revolution, Joanna had witnessed the transformation of the political landscape in the American colonies. The years leading up to the war had been marked by protests, boycotts, and growing resistance to British rule, with events like the Boston Tea Party and the Intolerable Acts fueling the fires of revolution. The outbreak of hostilities in 1775, particularly after the battles of Lexington and Concord, signaled the beginning of armed rebellion. As the Revolution progressed, the line between patriots and loyalists became sharply drawn.

For Joanna and Richard, their support for the British Crown would have been rooted in both personal and ideological factors. Loyalists often saw their allegiance as a defense of order, tradition, and the rights of the Crown. They believed that the colonies were better off under British rule and feared the chaos and uncertainty that might come with an independent republic. Their ties to Britain, both through Richard's military service and Joanna's family connections, would have influenced their perspective. For Joanna, the political pressures of the era would have meant navigating difficult decisions about her family's safety and future.

Being a Loyalist in New York was not without risk. New York was a divided colony, with the patriots gaining strength in cities like Albany and New York City, while the Loyalists were concentrated in the rural areas and along the Hudson River. The Cartwrights' support for the British would have made them targets of the colonial rebels, who viewed Loyalists as traitors to the cause of liberty. Joanna's role as a mother and a wife would have been central to her decision-making during these difficult years. She had to consider the well-being of her children in a time when families were torn apart by political allegiance, and the social fabric was disintegrating.

In the midst of the conflict, Joanna and Richard likely had to make significant sacrifices. Loyalists were often harassed, their homes looted, or they were forced to flee to safer areas. Some Loyalists were even imprisoned or exiled for their beliefs. The Cartwrights' status as Loyalists likely placed them under constant threat, and they may have seen their property confiscated or their assets diminished as a result of their allegiance. The fear of persecution would have weighed heavily on Joanna, who had already weathered many personal losses throughout her life.

In response to this turmoil, many Loyalists, including the Cartwrights, fled to British-controlled territories after the war. For Joanna and Richard, this could have meant relocating to Canada, where many Loyalists were resettled after the conflict. The aftermath of the war saw the Loyalists receive land grants and support from the British government in exchange for their loyalty. Joanna's future, as well as that of her family, would have been shaped by this new chapter in British North America.

As a mother, Joanna would have been determined to protect her children from the dangers of the war, even if it meant leaving behind her home and the life she had known. The decision to remain loyal to the Crown would have brought with it hardship and sacrifice, but it also reflected Joanna's strong sense of duty and belief in the principles of the British government.

Living through the Revolution as a Loyalist was a life fraught with personal and political challenges. The Cartwrights' commitment to the British cause would have shaped their experiences during the war, and Joanna's resilience as a mother and matriarch would have been tested as she navigated the turbulent waters of loyalty, family, and survival. The Cartwrights' eventual relocation to Canada was the beginning of a new chapter in their lives, one that would be defined by the legacy of their loyalty to the British Crown and the uncertain future of the colonies in the wake of the Revolution.

---

HERE IS A GENEALOGY travel itinerary, incorporating the route through Amherst Island to Kingston, Ontario:

**Day 1: New York City, New York**

Morning:

- Start at Fraunces Tavern Museum: Explore the history of the American Revolution and the Loyalists' role in New York City. This historic site offers insights into the period and the challenges faced by Loyalists like Joanna and Richard Cartwright.

Afternoon:

- Visit the Museum of the American Revolution: Located in Philadelphia, this museum provides a comprehensive overview of the Revolution, including the experiences of Loyalists.

Evening:

- Walk through Lower Manhattan: Reflect on the historical significance of the area where many Loyalists lived and faced persecution.

**Day 2: Hudson River Valley, New York**

Morning:

- Travel to Kingston: Visit the Senate House State Historic Site, where you can learn about the early colonial history and the impact of the Revolution on the region.

Afternoon:

- Explore the Hudson River Valley: Drive along the scenic routes, stopping at historical markers and sites related to the Loyalist experience.

Evening:

- Stay in Albany: The capital of New York State, Albany was a significant location during the Revolution. Visit the Schuyler Mansion State Historic Site to understand more about the era.

## Day 3: Albany to Montreal, Quebec

Morning:

• Drive to Montreal: Follow the route that many Loyalists took when fleeing to Canada. The journey itself is a reflection of the hardships faced by families like the Cartwrights.

Afternoon:

• Visit the Château Ramezay: This historic site in Montreal offers insights into the Loyalist migration and settlement in Canada.

Evening:

• Explore Old Montreal: Walk through the historic streets and imagine the arrival of Loyalist families seeking refuge.

## Day 4: Montreal to Amherst Island, Ontario

Morning:

• Travel to Amherst Island: This island was a significant stop for many Loyalists on their way to Kingston. The ferry service from Millhaven Wharf to Stella Wharf on Amherst Island is a scenic and historically significant route

RESOURCE[133]

AFTERNOON:

• Explore Amherst Island: Visit local historical sites and learn about the Loyalist settlements on the island.

---

133. https://bing.com/

search?q=Loyalist+route+to+Kingston%2c+Ontario+via+Amherst+Island&form=SKPBOT

Evening:

• Stay on Amherst Island: Enjoy the peaceful surroundings and reflect on the journey of the Loyalists.

**Day 5: Amherst Island to Kingston, Ontario**

Morning:

• Ferry to Kingston: Continue the journey to Kingston, where many Loyalists, including Joanna and Richard Cartwright, eventually settled.

Afternoon:

• Visit the United Empire Loyalist Heritage Centre and Park: Located in Adolphustown, near Kingston, this site offers a deep dive into the history and contributions of Loyalists in Canada.

Evening:

• Explore Kingston: Walk through the historic downtown area and visit sites like Fort Henry, which played a role in the defense of the region.

**Day 6: Kingston to Toronto, Ontario**

Morning:

• Drive to Toronto: Follow the route along Lake Ontario, stopping at historical sites and markers along the way.

Afternoon:

• Visit the Black Creek Pioneer Village: This open-air museum in Toronto provides a glimpse into the lives of early settlers, including Loyalists.

Evening:

• Explore Toronto's Historic Sites: Walk through the Distillery District and other historic areas to understand the city's development and the role of Loyalists in its history.

**Day 7: Toronto to Niagara-on-the-Lake, Ontario**

Morning:

• Travel to Niagara-on-the-Lake: This town is rich in Loyalist history and offers numerous sites to explore.

Afternoon:

• Visit Fort George: Learn about the military history and the role of Loyalists in defending the region during the War of 1812.

Evening:

• Stroll through the Historic Town: Enjoy the well-preserved 19th-century architecture and reflect on the legacy of the Loyalists.

**Day 8: Niagara-on-the-Lake to Rideau Lakes, Ontario**

Morning:

• Drive to Rideau Lakes: This area is known for its beautiful landscapes and historical significance.

Afternoon:

• Explore the Rideau Canal: A UNESCO World Heritage Site, the canal was built by Loyalists and their descendants. Visit the locks and learn about the engineering marvels of the time

Loyalist Township[134]

---

134. https://www.loyalist.ca/en/index.aspx

EVENING:

• Relax by the Lakes: Enjoy the natural beauty and reflect on the journey of Joanna Beasley Cartwright and her family.

———

AT 56 YEARS OLD, JOANNA Beasley Cartwright witnessed the advent of a groundbreaking technological achievement—the successful flight of the first hot air balloon in 1783. While this event may have been distant from her immediate concerns as a mother, matriarch, and Loyalist, it marked a significant moment in the history of human innovation and exploration.

The flight of the hot air balloon by the Montgolfier brothers in France was a pivotal moment in the 18th century, showcasing humanity's drive to explore the skies. Though the Cartwright family, living in the aftermath of the American Revolution, would have been focused on rebuilding and adjusting to the new realities of life as Loyalists in a post-revolutionary world, Joanna would likely have heard about this remarkable achievement, especially as news of such events traveled quickly even to the colonies.

For Joanna, now living as a more mature woman, the launch of the balloon would have been one of many moments that contributed to the profound changes happening in the world around her. The late 18th century was a time of remarkable transitions—political, social, and technological. The American Revolution had already reshaped the colonies, and the Enlightenment was bringing new ideas about science, reason, and progress. This event, the first hot air balloon flight, would have symbolized the possibilities of human innovation and the boldness of the era.

Though Joanna was focused on her own family, the emotional and practical aspects of life as a Loyalist, and the upheavals of the previous decades, the success of the Montgolfiers' flight might have resonated with her in a symbolic way. Her life had spanned great challenges and immense change: from her youth in Albany to her marriage and motherhood, through the ravages of war, the loss of loved ones, and her relocation to British-controlled Canada. The flight of the hot air balloon was a testament to the forward momentum of history, and as Joanna entered her later years, she may have seen it as yet another reminder of the unpredictable future her children and grandchildren would face in a rapidly changing world.

By 1783, Joanna had lived through both personal and political revolutions. The flight of the balloon could have sparked reflection on how far humanity could go, whether in the quest for independence or the pursuit of new frontiers in science and exploration. Joanna, like many of her contemporaries, may have witnessed changes in her world that she never could have imagined in her youth, including the rapid spread of new technologies and ideas. The hot air balloon, rising into the sky, could have been a metaphor for the turbulent history she had experienced and the hope for progress that would continue to unfold for her descendants.

As a mother, matriarch, and Loyalist, Joanna had always balanced the demands of family with the pressures of an ever-changing political landscape. The flight of the hot air balloon marked a moment of excitement in a world that was often defined by struggles and survival. While Joanna's life had been marked by personal losses and upheaval, she might have seen the balloon as an inspiring achievement—proof that even amidst chaos and uncertainty, there was room for human ingenuity to soar.

AT 63 YEARS OLD, JOANNA Beasley Cartwright experienced another personal loss when her half-brother, James Parker Van

Benthuysen, passed away in Albany in 1790. James had been part of Joanna's life for many years, as he was her half-brother from her mother Lydia Dally's previous marriage. His death would have marked yet another chapter in Joanna's ongoing process of grief and adjustment as she aged, losing family members one by one.

James, who had lived through the turbulence of the Revolution and the early years of the United States, would have been a familiar figure in Joanna's life. Like her, he had seen the dramatic changes brought about by the war and the shifting allegiances of the colonies. If Joanna and James had remained close over the years, his passing would have added to the weight of sorrow she had already borne—having lost her mother, father, and other loved ones over the past decades.

At this stage in her life, Joanna was likely reflecting on the impermanence of time. She had already experienced the trials of the American Revolution, the relocation to British-controlled Canada, and the loss of both family and home. Now, she faced the loss of another family member, a reminder of the passage of time and the fading of the old ways of life.

James's death in Albany also signified the ongoing changes in the region. Albany, once a key center of colonial administration and commerce, was shifting as the United States began to establish its new government. Joanna, who had been born in Albany and lived through so much of its history, would have had mixed feelings about the changes, perhaps feeling nostalgia for a time before the Revolution when Albany was a more stable and prosperous city.

Her own life, marked by her allegiance to the British Crown, had placed Joanna on a path far different from those who had supported the American cause. She had borne the scars of loyalty to the Crown—through her losses during the Revolution, her forced relocation, and the difficulties of being a Loyalist in a post-Revolutionary world. The death of her half-brother, James, would likely have been another sorrowful reminder of how much had changed and how many of her generation were passing away.

Joanna's response to the death of James Parker Van Benthuysen would have been one of reflection, perhaps recalling the days when the Van Benthuysen family had been a more prominent presence in Albany. She would also have been contemplating the future of her own children and grandchildren, as the world around them continued to evolve rapidly. This loss would have made Joanna more aware of the importance of family bonds and legacies—her own family's history, both before and after the Revolution.

As Joanna entered her later years, this loss could have spurred her to reflect on her own legacy. She had lived through extraordinary times, and her life had been marked by change, loss, and survival. The passing of James, like the deaths of so many before him, would have been a poignant reminder of the fleeting nature of life. Yet, she likely found solace in the family she had raised and the strength she had shown as a mother, wife, and matriarch during turbulent times.

AT 68 YEARS OLD, JOANNA Beasley Cartwright faced the profound loss of her husband, Richard Cartwright I, who passed away in Kingston, Upper Canada, on October 23, 1794. This marked a significant moment in her life, as Richard had been her partner for nearly five decades, and his death would have brought an overwhelming sense of finality to the long journey they had shared.

Richard and Joanna had lived through tumultuous times, from the early days of their marriage in Albany to their relocation to Upper Canada as Loyalists following the American Revolution. As one of the most prominent Loyalist families, their life together had been filled with the trials and sacrifices of their political allegiance, as well as the challenges of starting anew in a foreign land. Joanna would have shared in the rebuilding of their lives in Kingston, a city that had grown in importance during the post-Revolutionary era, serving as the capital of Upper Canada at the time.

The loss of her husband would have marked the end of an era for Joanna. They had weathered many storms together, including the upheaval of war, the loss of their ancestral home, and the long journey north to the British-held territories. Their shared experiences as Loyalists, trying to rebuild and secure a future for their children and descendants in the new British colonies, were now a part of history.

Richard's death in 1794 would also have marked the beginning of Joanna's life without him by her side, a new phase where she would have to navigate the challenges of aging alone and relying more on her children and their families. By this time, Joanna had seen much of her family grow up and start their own lives. Many of her children, now adults, would have been pillars of support for her in the wake of Richard's passing.

Kingston, as the seat of government for Upper Canada, was a rapidly evolving place. Joanna, as a woman who had lived through such transformative events in both the colonies and the newly established Canadian territories, would have been keenly aware of how the political landscape was shifting. Despite the loss of her husband, she would have seen her children and grandchildren thriving in this new world.

Joanna's grief over Richard's passing would have been profound, but as a matriarch who had already endured much in her lifetime, she would also have found strength in her family. She had survived the loss of loved ones, the dislocation from her homeland, and the political upheaval of the Revolution. Richard's death, while a deep sorrow, would not have been her first experience with loss, and she had likely come to understand the resilience needed to carry on.

Her mourning would have been intertwined with a sense of duty to her family's legacy—continuing the work that Richard and she had started as Loyalists in this new land. Joanna had raised children who were part of the fabric of this new world, and though the loss of Richard left an undeniable void, she would have found purpose in helping to shape the future of the Cartwright family in the years to come.

In the aftermath of her husband's death, Joanna's life would have been one of reflection and transition, surrounded by the family she had worked so hard to build and sustain. As the family matriarch, she would have remained an important figure in Kingston, a witness to the ongoing development of the region and a link to the past for her descendants.

JOANNA BEASLEY CARTWRIGHT passed away in Kingston, Upper Canada, in 1795, at the age of 69, just a year after the death of her beloved husband, Richard Cartwright I. Her passing marked the end of an era for the Cartwright family, and she was laid to rest alongside him in St. Paul's Anglican Churchyard, the final resting place of many of Kingston's early settlers.

By this time, Joanna had lived through a lifetime of upheaval and transformation—from her birth in Albany in 1726 to her family's forced relocation to Canada as Loyalists after the American Revolution. She had witnessed the birth of a new nation and the establishment of British Canada, navigating both the joys and hardships of life in a new land. Joanna's life had been marked by devotion to her family, resilience in the face of adversity, and a deep commitment to her Loyalist ideals.

Her burial in St. Paul's Anglican Churchyard, alongside Richard, symbolized the family's lasting presence in Kingston, a city that had grown to be the heart of Upper Canada. The church, which had long been an important spiritual and community center, stood as a testament to the Cartwrights' commitment to their faith and their new life in Canada. Being buried together in this prominent location was also a recognition of their legacy and the significant role they had played in the Loyalist settlement and the early years of the British colonial period in Canada.

Joanna's death in 1795, only a year after Richard's, suggested that she may have been deeply affected by his passing. The two had been married for nearly half a century, enduring the tumult of war, exile, and settlement in a new land. Joanna, now surrounded by children, grandchildren, and the community they had helped build in Kingston, would have found some solace in knowing that her family had carried on the work she and Richard had started, forging a new life in Upper Canada.

Her legacy lived on not just in her children, who had grown into respected members of the Loyalist community, but also in the strength and resilience she had passed down. She had seen the next generation of Cartwrights settle into their place in the new world, and although she did not live to see the future unfold, her life had shaped the family's story and the development of the region.

Joanna Beasley Cartwright's resting place, beside Richard in St. Paul's Anglican Churchyard, was a final reflection of her enduring connection to her family, her faith, and the community she had helped to establish. Her life was a testament to survival, adaptation, and the persistence of loyalty—values that had carried her through the trials of war, the loss of homeland, and the challenges of establishing a new life in Canada.

Her memory, like her husband's, would continue to be honored by her descendants in the generations that followed.

---

HERE'S A GENEALOGY travel itinerary that traces the life and legacy of Joanna Beasley Cartwright, focusing on her journey from Albany to Kingston, Upper Canada:

**Day 1: Albany, New York**

Morning:

• Start at the Albany Institute of History & Art: Explore exhibits on the colonial history of Albany, where Joanna was born in 1726.

Afternoon:

• Visit the Schuyler Mansion State Historic Site: Learn about the prominent families and the political landscape of Albany during Joanna's early years.

Evening:

• Walk through Historic Downtown Albany: Reflect on the early life of Joanna and the colonial atmosphere of the 18th century.

**Day 2: New York City, New York**

Morning:

• Travel to New York City: Visit the Fraunces Tavern Museum to understand the Loyalist perspective during the American Revolution.

Afternoon:

• Explore the Museum of the American Revolution: Located in Philadelphia, this museum provides a comprehensive overview of the Revolution, including the experiences of Loyalists.

Evening:

• Walk through Lower Manhattan: Reflect on the historical significance of the area where many Loyalists lived and faced persecution.

**Day 3: Hudson River Valley, New York**

Morning:

• Travel to Kingston: Visit the Senate House State Historic Site to learn about the early colonial history and the impact of the Revolution on the region.

Afternoon:

• Explore the Hudson River Valley: Drive along the scenic routes, stopping at historical markers and sites related to the Loyalist experience.

Evening:

• Stay in Albany: The capital of New York State, Albany was a significant location during the Revolution. Visit the Schuyler Mansion State Historic Site to understand more about the era.

**Day 4: Albany to Montreal, Quebec**

Morning:

• Drive to Montreal: Follow the route that many Loyalists took when fleeing to Canada. The journey itself is a reflection of the hardships faced by families like the Cartwrights.

Afternoon:

• Visit the Château Ramezay: This historic site in Montreal offers insights into the Loyalist migration and settlement in Canada.

Evening:

• Explore Old Montreal: Walk through the historic streets and imagine the arrival of Loyalist families seeking refuge.

## Day 5: Montreal to Amherst Island, Ontario

Morning:

• Travel to Amherst Island: This island was a significant stop for many Loyalists on their way to Kingston. The ferry service from Millhaven Wharf to Stella Wharf on Amherst Island is a scenic and historically significant route

RESOURCE[135]

AFTERNOON:

• Explore Amherst Island: Visit local historical sites and learn about the Loyalist settlements on the island.

Evening:

• Stay on Amherst Island: Enjoy the peaceful surroundings and reflect on the journey of the Loyalists.

## Day 6: Amherst Island to Kingston, Ontario

Morning:

---

135. https://uelac.ca/loyalist-books/tracing-loyalist-ancestors-upper-canada/

- Ferry to Kingston: Continue the journey to Kingston, where many Loyalists, including Joanna and Richard Cartwright, eventually settled.

Afternoon:

- Visit St. Paul's Anglican Churchyard: Pay respects at the final resting place of Joanna and Richard Cartwright. Reflect on their contributions to the Loyalist community in Kingston.

Evening:

- Explore Kingston: Walk through the historic downtown area and visit sites like Fort Henry, which played a role in the defense of the region.

**Day 7: Kingston, Ontario**

Morning:

- Visit the United Empire Loyalist Heritage Centre and Park: Located in Adolphustown, near Kingston, this site offers a deep dive into the history and contributions of Loyalists in Canada.

Afternoon:

- Explore the Kingston Penitentiary: Learn about the history of the penitentiary and its connections to the early settlers of Kingston.

Evening:

- Stroll along the Waterfront: Enjoy the scenic views of Lake Ontario and reflect on the legacy of the Loyalists in Kingston.

**Day 8: Kingston to Rideau Lakes, Ontario**

Morning:

• Drive to Rideau Lakes: This area is known for its beautiful landscapes and historical significance.

Afternoon:

• Explore the Rideau Canal: A UNESCO World Heritage Site, the canal was built by Loyalists and their descendants. Visit the locks and learn about the engineering marvels of the time

Land Boards of Upper Canada, 1765-1804 - Library and Archives Canada[136]

EVENING:

• Relax by the Lakes: Enjoy the natural beauty and reflect on the journey of Joanna Beasley Cartwright and her family.

---

136. https://www.bac-lac.gc.ca/eng/discover/land/land-boards-upper-canada/Pages/

land-boards-upper-canada.aspx

# RICHARD CARTWRIGHT UE[5]

When Richard Cartwright I was born in Colton, Staffordshire, on October 18, 1720, England was a nation deeply embedded in the early years of the Georgian period. This era was marked by the reign of King George I (who ascended in 1714) and was a time of cultural, scientific, and economic evolution for the country.

Life in Colton, a small village in Staffordshire, would have reflected a rural England just beginning to feel the ripples of the upcoming Industrial Revolution. The area was largely agricultural, with farming and pastoral work dominating the local economy. Villages like Colton were tightly knit communities, often with families living in the same place for generations, maintaining close relationships through shared land, trade, and the parish church, which was the social and spiritual center of village life.

Social and Economic Landscape

In the early 18th century, England was experiencing economic growth, especially in trade, driven by its colonial ambitions. This was the age of mercantilism, where commerce, particularly the wool and textile industries, was steadily expanding. However, this prosperity was often concentrated in the growing cities rather than in the rural regions, where many villagers lived as tenant farmers, laborers, or craftsmen. Although there was a push toward urbanization and industry, the people of Colton would still have led largely agrarian lives, adhering to traditional seasonal rhythms for planting, harvesting, and local fairs.

The Influence of the Church

Religion was a central aspect of life in 1720, especially in smaller communities like Colton, where the Anglican Church played a foundational role. Almost everyone in the village would have attended church regularly, with Sundays marked by sermons and gatherings that not only fostered community but also reinforced social expectations and religious devotion. The church's influence extended to education, moral guidance, and even local governance.

Family and Community

In Richard Cartwright's time, family was the core unit of society, and large families were typical. Families worked together on farms or in family-owned businesses, and children were raised to contribute to the household from an early age. Men, particularly those from well-connected or skilled backgrounds, might move between trades, learning skills such as carpentry, blacksmithing, or even clerical work in nearby towns. For families with some wealth or connections, an education might be possible, often limited to basic literacy, arithmetic, and religious studies for most boys, though some would attend grammar schools.

Education and Enlightenment Ideas

While Colton itself would have been largely removed from the cultural shifts of the time, the broader intellectual climate was changing. This period was the dawn of the Enlightenment, where ideas about science, reason, and individual rights were spreading across Europe. Though these ideas were more prevalent among the urban middle and upper classes, they were starting to challenge established institutions and, eventually, would shape policies and social movements in England.

Georgian Social Hierarchy and Status

Richard Cartwright was born into a world with a rigid social hierarchy. England was a class-conscious society, where one's birth and family connections largely determined opportunities and status. The landed gentry, who owned the majority of land, held considerable power and influence. Below them were yeomen and tenant farmers, like many in Staffordshire, who worked the land and owed duties to their landlords. The lower classes, including laborers and servants, had fewer opportunities, although some would find ways to improve their circumstances through trade or skilled labor.

As a young man from Staffordshire, Richard would have had limited upward mobility, but the times were beginning to change. If his family were skilled or connected enough, there might be chances for advancement, either by seeking opportunities in towns, where trade and craftsmanship were thriving, or eventually, by emigrating to the colonies, where new opportunities were emerging.

Global Context

In 1720, England was a burgeoning empire with colonies in America, the Caribbean, and Asia. The country's wealth and influence were expanding, though it faced competition from France, Spain, and the Dutch. This era saw the British Navy asserting its dominance on the seas, ensuring England's continued prosperity through trade. This colonial reach would soon influence many English families, including Cartwright's, who, generations later, would find themselves in North America amid colonial ambitions and conflict.

In summary, Richard Cartwright I was born into a world marked by rural life, traditional structures, and the beginnings of a shift in thought and economy. He came into a society where religion, family, and local community shaped daily life, and England's expanding colonial empire would open new paths for families willing to venture into the unknown—a choice he and his family would ultimately make in the years that followed.

RICHARD CARTWRIGHT I was 18 years old in 1738 when the Methodist movement emerged as a powerful religious and social force within England. That year, John and Charles Wesley, alongside George Whitefield, experienced religious awakenings that led to the foundation of Methodism, a movement within the Church of England. Although it began as a reform movement, it would eventually develop into a distinct denomination.

Early Methodist Movement and Religious Tension

The Methodists emphasized personal faith, moral discipline, and social outreach, attracting followers from all social classes, especially among the poor and working class. They often preached outdoors to reach a broader audience, something unheard of and even frowned upon at the time. Traditional Anglican leaders were skeptical of the new movement, viewing it as disruptive and even radical.

Impact on Society and the Working Class

For people like Richard Cartwright, who came from the working and middle classes, Methodism provided a message that emphasized individual worth, social justice, and a personal relationship with God. This message was especially appealing to those who felt overlooked by the traditional structures of the Anglican Church. It offered a spiritual alternative, one that encouraged both self-improvement and a sense of belonging within a more personal religious community.

In rural Staffordshire, the Methodist message could have begun to reach individuals through traveling preachers and word-of-mouth. Even though Cartwright himself may not have converted, the Methodist movement would have been seen as part of the changing religious landscape, bringing a renewed focus on social issues, morality, and inclusivity.

## Methodist Values and the Cultural Climate

Methodism's emphasis on discipline and community resonated with the social values of the time, encouraging thrift, hard work, and charity—virtues that were especially valued among the Protestant working and middle classes. By promoting Bible study, literacy, and temperance, Methodism aligned with many of the ideals of the Enlightenment, blending faith with a sense of moral responsibility. These values often conflicted with England's elite, who saw the movement as subversive, but for common people, they were empowering.

## Potential Influence on Cartwright's Future

Although Methodism wouldn't fully take root until later in the century, its early growth would subtly influence the lives of young men like Cartwright, especially if he later encountered Methodists in the colonies. As a future Loyalist who would live through the American Revolution and later settle in Upper Canada, the principles of self-discipline and commitment to a higher cause may have resonated with him, even if he remained Anglican. The movement's rise would underscore the importance of personal conviction and commitment—qualities that would also define the Loyalist spirit during the Revolution.

## Methodism and the Seeds of Social Reform

Methodism's foundation came at a time when England's social inequalities were increasingly visible, laying early seeds for reform. In an era marked by rigid class distinctions, Methodism offered an alternative that prioritized inclusivity and community service, challenging the status quo. The movement's messages of social justice and equality would eventually shape moral discussions across England, influencing attitudes toward charity, education, and even the rights of workers and enslaved individuals.

Thus, at age 18, Richard Cartwright was witness to the birth of a movement that would eventually reshape England's religious and social landscapes, foreshadowing the social changes that he and his descendants would experience in North America. While he may have viewed Methodism as a novel, perhaps controversial religious movement, its ideas of morality, social responsibility, and dedication would have quietly mirrored the virtues that would come to define his Loyalist beliefs.

RICHARD CARTWRIGHT was 22 years old when he married Joanna Beasley on July 12, 1743, in Albany, New York. This was a time when Albany was a bustling center of trade and diplomacy in the northern British colonies, situated on the frontier of the British Empire. While it had long been a stronghold of Dutch influence from its colonial beginnings, by the 1740s, Albany had transitioned fully under British control, creating a blend of English and Dutch cultures in its architecture, customs, and community life. For Cartwright, this marriage marked not only the start of his family but also his formal integration into the diverse and industrious colonial society of New York.

Albany in the 1740s: A Strategic Trade Hub

Albany, positioned along the Hudson River, was a vital port and trading post linking the British colonies with Indigenous nations to the north and west. This was the heart of the fur trade, with British and Dutch traders exchanging goods with Indigenous nations, such as the Haudenosaunee (Iroquois Confederacy), for furs. Albany's economy depended heavily on these alliances, and many of its residents—particularly prominent families—held significant roles as intermediaries between the colonial government and Indigenous groups.

The community itself was tight-knit and often resistant to the rapid changes brought by British rule. For someone like Richard Cartwright, entering into married life here meant adapting to Albany's mix of Dutch, British, and Indigenous influences and navigating the complexities of colonial politics and trade.

Social and Cultural Expectations in Marriage

In 18th-century Albany, marriage was a significant social institution that helped forge alliances, secure family connections, and strengthen one's social standing. The Cartwrights, like many young couples of the time, would have entered into marriage with an understanding of these obligations. Families were expected to support one another, not only in daily life but also in terms of reputation and loyalty within the community.

Colonial Albany's social structure was hierarchical, with a marked difference between the affluent merchants, who often dominated local government, and the laborers and tradespeople. Marriages within such a community played an essential role in defining social status and cementing one's place within the wider colonial network. For the Cartwrights, this meant embracing the social customs of both Dutch and English heritages in Albany, including hosting community events, attending church, and raising their children within these cultural norms.

Challenges and Frontier Realities

Albany in the 1740s was, in many ways, a frontier town, with all the associated challenges and unpredictability. Although fortified, it was still vulnerable to raids and skirmishes due to its location on the edge of

British-held territory. Conflicts with the French and their Indigenous allies in Canada made the region tense and prone to violence, which would escalate into the French and Indian War in the following decade. For young couples like Richard and Joanna, these tensions would have added an element of uncertainty to their lives, as every aspect of daily living—from securing goods to maintaining family safety—was influenced by the region's volatility.

Daily Life in a Frontier Marriage

As newlyweds, the Cartwrights would have settled into the routines of colonial life, balancing home responsibilities, economic activities, and social obligations. Men like Richard were typically involved in trade, skilled labor, or even farming, depending on family connections and resources. Women managed households, raised children, and participated in community and church events. Colonial marriages were partnerships out of necessity, as survival often depended on both spouses contributing to the household's upkeep.

Albany's multicultural environment also influenced domestic life. English-speaking families like the Cartwrights would often find themselves interacting with Dutch and Indigenous neighbors, adopting and adapting various customs. Women were central to this cultural exchange, often learning new recipes, herbal remedies, and household management techniques from their neighbors.

The Start of a Family

For Richard and Joanna, beginning their married life in Albany marked the start of a new family legacy. As the couple's family grew, each child would represent a new connection to Albany's social and economic fabric. Their children's births would have been celebrated within the community, with each baptism, church service, and family event strengthening the family's standing.

Richard Cartwright's marriage to Joanna in Albany in 1743 thus placed him at the heart of colonial life in one of the most strategic towns of the British Empire in North America. The frontier tensions, blended culture, and tight-knit community of Albany would shape his early years and lay the groundwork for his journey from a young English immigrant to a loyalist settler, eventually resettling in Upper Canada with his wife and family.

WHEN RICHARD CARTWRIGHT was 26 years old, he and Joanna welcomed their first child, John, on July 12, 1747, in Albany, New York. This moment marked Richard's official entry into fatherhood, adding new responsibilities and joys to his life. As Albany was a small but tightly connected community, the birth of a first son would have been a significant event, not only for the Cartwright family but also for the larger social circle around them. In 18th-century colonial life, sons were especially prized as heirs who could carry on the family name, responsibilities, and trade.

Raising a Son in Colonial Albany

For Richard, raising a son in Albany would have carried unique expectations, especially in a town deeply influenced by both British and Dutch traditions. From the start, John would have been woven into the customs and values of this multicultural colonial society, where trade, negotiation, and alliance-building were central skills. Richard's role would have included teaching John the essentials of being an upright member of the community, preparing him to one day handle family responsibilities and, possibly, follow in his father's footsteps in trade or another profession.

Albany's Colonial Community and the Next Generation

Richard and Joanna, like other colonial parents, would have been eager to instill values that reflected the beliefs of the Anglican Church and the British crown, as loyalty was crucial in these times of shifting alliances and frontier conflicts. As a family of Loyalist leanings, the Cartwrights would eventually experience both privilege and risk, especially as political tensions began to mount with Britain's increased control over the colonies. This environment meant that young John would have been raised amid discussions of loyalty, governance, and civic duty, all of which his parents would have felt strongly about.

Expectations of Sons in Colonial Society

In this period, the eldest son was often expected to learn the family's trade, manage family affairs, and become a central figure in supporting parents as they aged. As the Cartwrights' firstborn, John was likely the focus of these expectations from an early age. For Richard, this would mean balancing the role of father, mentor, and community member, passing on his values, beliefs, and work ethic to his son.

Moreover, as Albany was still very much a town on the edge of wilderness, practical skills would have been essential. Young boys in Albany grew up learning skills relevant to both town and frontier life: carpentry, agriculture, and even defensive tactics were part of a standard colonial education.

The Impact of Albany's Social and Political Climate

The late 1740s were marked by ongoing colonial tensions and shifting alliances, notably with the Indigenous nations and the French to the north. Albany's location on the Hudson River made it a critical military and trading outpost, where residents often felt the impact of these conflicts more acutely than those in other colonies. Raising a son like John in this environment would mean preparing him for a life in a region where colonial politics, Indigenous relations, and the constant movement of goods and people all held sway.

The birth of John Cartwright in 1747 would set the Cartwright family on a path that would eventually take them far from Albany, to Kingston in Upper Canada. Through his son's arrival, Richard's life would be reshaped by the hopes and responsibilities of fatherhood, shaping not only his personal legacy but also helping to define a Loyalist legacy that would carry the Cartwright name across borders and into a new chapter of North American history.

WHEN RICHARD CARTWRIGHT was 27 years old, he and Joanna welcomed their second child, a daughter named Susanna, born in 1748 in Albany, New York. The addition of a daughter brought a new dynamic into the Cartwright household, as daughters in colonial society held a unique and often complex role. While sons were expected to carry on family names and trades, daughters were valued for the connections they might bring through marriage and for their integral role in family life, culture, and household duties.

Life for a Daughter in 18th-Century Albany

Susanna's early years would have been shaped by the rhythms of colonial domestic life, including household chores, early schooling, and learning the social customs expected of young women. As Albany was a town influenced by British and Dutch customs, girls often received education in both home management and basic literacy, especially among families with social standing. For the Cartwrights, the family's loyalty to British governance would also mean that Susanna's upbringing was steeped in Anglican faith, and she would likely attend church with her family at St. Peter's Anglican Church, which had been established in 1715.

Women's Role and Expectations

For young girls like Susanna, life in the mid-18th century carried with it the expectation that they would contribute significantly to their household, learning everything from cooking and sewing to hospitality. The household economy was essential in colonial life, and girls were often brought up to manage complex households, especially if they were expected to marry into families involved in trade or politics. Susanna would also be expected to adopt the values of modesty, duty, and loyalty, attributes prized in the colonial culture of her family.

A Social Life Marked by Community and Faith

In a small but bustling community like Albany, a young girl's social world would be rich in both family and communal interactions. Susanna likely had frequent opportunities to mix with other children in the tight-knit community, as social gatherings, religious events, and market days were central to community life. These connections were especially valuable in a place like Albany, where families often shared deep generational ties to the land and to each other.

The Cartwright Family's Loyalist Leanings and Future Challenges

While Susanna's early years were likely marked by relative peace and security, the Cartwright family's Loyalist views would later place them at odds with many neighbors as tensions rose between Britain and its colonies. Growing up, Susanna would have heard her father and mother discussing issues like trade restrictions, British taxes, and the colonial assemblies' grievances. For a young girl, these political conversations were a window into the divisions taking shape in her world—a conflict that would ultimately lead the Cartwright family to relocate to Upper Canada as part of the Loyalist migration.

Susanna's birth expanded the Cartwright household, filling it with the joys and responsibilities that accompanied the raising of both sons and daughters in the colonial period. For Richard, his daughter represented both a beloved family member and a future bridge to Albany's tightly connected families, many of whom would soon face a crossroads as revolutionary sentiments swept through the colonies.

---

WHEN RICHARD CARTWRIGHT was 29 years old, he and Joanna welcomed their third child, Elizabeth, into the world on May 13, 1750, in New York Colony. By this time, the Cartwrights were a well-established family in Albany, navigating both the demands of raising young children and the responsibilities of Richard's career. With Elizabeth's birth, their family life would grow even busier, as daughters in colonial households were often involved in daily home duties from a young age, learning to uphold and perpetuate family values and traditions.

The Role of Daughters in a Colonial Family

As Elizabeth grew, she would begin learning the skills expected of young girls, preparing her for a future where marriage and household management were both a duty and a significant role. In Richard and Joanna's household, Elizabeth's upbringing would likely have emphasized the importance of faith, family honor, and the particular skills needed to contribute to a family deeply rooted in Loyalist ideals. As the political landscape in the colonies became more tense, families like the Cartwrights raised their daughters with the knowledge that loyalty to British rule might soon have greater consequences.

Growing Up in a Town Divided

For Elizabeth, Albany in the 1750s was a town filled with complex relationships—between the British colonists, the Dutch settlers, the Native American nations, and the growing colonial dissatisfaction with British authority. Though she was young, Elizabeth's early years were surrounded by conversations about these divisions, which must have touched every part of Albany society. The Cartwright family's Loyalist leanings would have added further complexity, as many neighbors and friends around them began to express discontent with British rule.

Education and Social Training

While formal schooling for girls in the 18th century was limited, Elizabeth would have received a practical education at home. Her mother, Joanna, would have taught her to read and write, as well as skills essential to maintaining a well-run household. By the time she was old enough to take on more responsibility, Elizabeth would be proficient in the essential arts of cooking, sewing, managing servants, and understanding family accounts, skills that were crucial for women in colonial society, especially if they were to marry into a family of standing or means.

Elizabeth's arrival would have brought a new light to the Cartwright family, but also the duty of preparing her for a future that was uncertain. As tensions continued to rise in the colonies, Elizabeth's parents likely faced the challenge of raising her with an awareness of loyalty and duty to the crown, even as those around them grew restless. For Richard, the birth of Elizabeth underscored his role as both a father and a figure in Albany's Loyalist community—one who would one day help lead his family to a new life in Upper Canada as Loyalist refugees.

RICHARD CARTWRIGHT was 36 years old when his daughter Susannah was born in New York Colony, with her christening recorded on September 4, 1757. With her arrival, the Cartwright family continued to grow, reinforcing their close bonds amid the backdrop of political tensions and impending change. Like her older sister, Susanna, who had been born nearly a decade prior, Susannah would have been raised with the same strong Loyalist principles that would later influence her family's future.

Naming Customs and Family Bonds

Naming a daughter Susannah, so similar to her elder sister Susanna, was a notable choice, possibly reflecting both tradition and the emotional resonance of names within the family. It's possible that the name was chosen in honor of her older sister, who may have died young or had a particularly special place in the family's hearts. Colonial families often reused names to memorialize a child or uphold a cherished family connection, which could explain why the Cartwrights chose a name so similar to that of their first daughter. This custom highlighted the significance of family continuity and remembrance, especially during an era where child mortality was high.

The Challenges of Colonial Motherhood

For Joanna, the birth of Susannah marked yet another period of tending to an infant, along with caring for a growing household. In colonial society, the presence of younger siblings created natural bonds and often laid the foundation for strong family loyalties and interdependence. As she grew, Susannah would become a companion to her siblings, sharing in both household tasks and play, which were essential parts of childhood in the colonial era.

Life in New York Colony in the 1750s

Susannah's birth occurred during an era marked by both growth and tension in the colonies. The French and Indian War (1754–1763) was underway, bringing conflict to the frontier regions and impacting colonial life profoundly. Albany, being a strategically important location, saw increased military presence and was a hub of activity as British and colonial forces moved against French territories and sought alliances with Indigenous nations.

Growing up in Albany during this time meant that young Susannah would be surrounded by reminders of Britain's struggle to control North America. Her early years were likely filled with stories of battles, fortifications, and news of soldiers passing through, creating a backdrop of uncertainty for the future. For her parents, who were staunch Loyalists, the war was both a defense of their British identity and a cause for concern, as political changes could alter their own lives and livelihoods in ways they could only anticipate.

Loyalist Values and Family Stability

By the time Susannah was born, Richard and Joanna had been married for nearly fifteen years, giving them experience and stability in raising a family in a turbulent time. They would have instilled in Susannah the importance of loyalty to the crown, religious devotion, and respect for family hierarchy. In a world where political allegiances were shifting rapidly, the Cartwrights aimed to anchor their children with values that would hold strong, no matter the challenges ahead.

As Richard continued his work and strengthened his standing in the Loyalist community, Susannah's early years were spent in a household that was as much a refuge as it was a place of learning and growth. Each of Richard and Joanna's children would soon be shaped by their commitment to loyalty and duty, values that would ultimately lead them northward to Upper Canada, where their allegiance would find a new home in a young, burgeoning society.

RICHARD CARTWRIGHT was 33 when the French and Indian War ignited in 1754, marking the beginning of a brutal struggle for North American dominance between Britain and France. For Richard, a Loyalist deeply rooted in British allegiance, the conflict was more than a distant frontier skirmish; it was a defense of his homeland's interests in the colonies and a reaffirmation of the British crown's reach.

Albany on the Edge of War

As the war unfolded, Albany, strategically positioned along the Hudson River, became an essential military and logistical hub for British operations. The town saw a constant flow of soldiers, supplies, and news of battles won and lost. This transformation heightened the bustling nature of Albany, but it also brought anxiety as the threat of violence edged closer. Richard, with a young and growing family, would have been acutely aware of the potential dangers nearby, yet would likely have felt a strong sense of duty to support the British cause.

The Cartwright Family's Perspective on the War

Richard's family was now woven into the fabric of a community divided by loyalties and impacted by the harsh realities of war. The French and Indian War was a conflict not only between European powers but also one that involved various Native American tribes, each aligning with different sides for their own survival and autonomy. For a Loyalist like Richard, the war represented a clash of cultures and powers in which he felt compelled to side with the British, seeing it as both a defense of his values and his family's future.

Economic and Personal Impact

While Albany grew as a staging ground for British military action, local economies adapted to the needs of the war, and merchants were called upon to provide goods and services for the military. Richard may have had economic opportunities in this environment, as many Loyalist families found ways to support the British war effort, either through provisioning or providing strategic information. However, the demands of wartime also meant increased taxes, disrupted trade routes, and the looming possibility of conscription or recruitment.

In 1756, just two years into the war, Albany itself was on high alert as nearby Fort Oswego fell to the French, sending waves of fear through the colonies. Though Richard was not a soldier, the atmosphere of Albany would have been heavy with the sounds of military drills, the sight of fortifications, and the shared tension among families. The security of his family—and his Loyalist convictions—became more pressing concerns amid a conflict that was reshaping colonial society.

Family Life Amid Conflict

With young children to care for, including newborns Susanna and Elizabeth, the war likely had a significant impact on family routines. Richard's wife, Joanna, would have shouldered much of the burden of maintaining a stable household amid wartime disruptions. They had already faced the challenges of raising a family in a bustling, occasionally divided town; now, the war brought both pride and peril to their daily lives.

For the Cartwrights, the French and Indian War would be remembered not just as a political event but as an era of resilience. Richard's experiences during this time, his exposure to the harsh realities of colonial warfare, and his deepening Loyalist identity would influence his decisions and ultimately guide his family toward Upper Canada when the American Revolution later engulfed the colonies.

IN 1754, THE SAME YEAR the French and Indian War erupted, Richard's family welcomed a new daughter, Catherine. Her arrival would have been a moment of joy amidst the gathering storm of war. The birth of a child brought a reminder of life's continuity and hope for the future, even as the world around them grew more uncertain.

A Newborn Amidst Unrest

For Richard and Joanna, balancing the excitement of a newborn with the challenges of a wartime environment demanded strength and adaptability. Albany, filled with the movement of soldiers and the demands of the British military, was not an easy place to raise a growing family. The news of British victories and defeats trickled in alongside whispers of Native American alliances and rumors of potential attacks. Yet, despite the looming dangers, Richard and Joanna likely saw Catherine's birth as an affirmation of their commitment to their family and to the ideals they held as Loyalists.

## Catherine's World

Catherine would grow up in a household rooted in Loyalist principles, surrounded by the stories and tensions of a British colonial town on the brink of upheaval. Even as an infant, she became part of the Cartwrights' shared journey—one that would eventually lead her far from Albany. Her earliest years would have been spent in a bustling, complex environment where the British military presence was strong, and the divide between Loyalists and those with Patriot sympathies would have been increasingly evident.

## The Family's Legacy and Loyalty

As a Loyalist, Richard would have felt all the more determined to raise his children with a sense of duty and attachment to the British Crown, seeing it as a source of stability in their lives. While his young daughter Catherine would have little awareness of the turmoil around her, her birth during such a pivotal year symbolized the future that Richard and Joanna hoped to preserve—a future that included their values, traditions, and loyalty to Britain. It's likely that Catherine, along with her siblings, would grow up hearing her father's stories of loyalty and heritage, which would later influence her own identity as the family faced new challenges.

Resilience in the Face of War

The birth of Catherine also strengthened the Cartwright family's resilience. Richard and Joanna had to adapt quickly, sheltering their children from the immediate dangers while staying informed and prepared for what might come next. The family would witness the French and Indian War shape the colonies profoundly, as the British, French, and Native American tribes clashed over control of lands and resources. This turbulent period would mold the Cartwrights' family dynamic and instill in them a fierce sense of unity and perseverance, traits that would carry them through even more dramatic changes in the decades to come.

The birth of Catherine in 1754 marked a turning point, symbolizing both the continuation of family life and the Cartwrights' steadfast loyalty amidst the looming storms of war and revolution that would test them in every way.

AT 35, RICHARD WELCOMED his son Henry, born in New York City on December 7, 1755. Henry's birth would have brought additional purpose and resolve to Richard, who now had a family of six children depending on his guidance and protection. This was a time of heightened tension in the colonies, with the French and Indian War in full swing and the British Crown's presence looming large in everyday colonial life.

The Cartwrights' Increasing Sense of Duty

For Richard, the arrival of another son would have solidified his focus on creating a legacy of loyalty, security, and British identity. Having an ever-growing family likely reinforced his determination to shelter his children from the political strife and to instill in them a respect for British rule. Henry's birth meant that Richard now had two sons—John and Henry—who could potentially carry forward his values and his legacy, and perhaps even follow him in serving the Crown.

## Life in a Divided Colony

The war not only brought conflict between British and French forces but also made New York a place of shifting allegiances and growing suspicion. Even among neighbors, the divide between those who supported the British and those who sympathized with the French grew sharper. Raising young children in this environment meant that Richard and Joanna had to be vigilant, not only for their safety but for their reputation as Loyalists. New York City itself was a major port and hub of commerce, but it was also becoming increasingly politically charged. For the Cartwrights, establishing themselves as steadfastly Loyalist meant forging a path that would lead to significant upheaval in the coming years, as loyalties fractured with the onset of the American Revolution.

## Family Dynamics and Responsibilities

As Henry grew from infant to child, Richard and Joanna would have faced the daily challenges of managing a household amid the pressures of war. The family's ever-growing size meant more responsibilities for each of them, as well as more mouths to feed and protect. Joanna, who had already raised four children during wartime, would have found her time and energies stretched as she balanced household duties with the need to teach her children about their heritage and the values she and Richard held dear.

## Preparing for an Uncertain Future

For Richard, Henry's birth likely underscored the need to think long-term. As war raged on, he would have wondered what kind of world his children, especially his sons, would inherit. In raising Henry,

Richard would have sought to prepare him for a future in which British influence was expected to remain dominant, yet he could already sense that the colonies were entering a period of profound change. Unknowingly, this preparation for colonial life would soon be redirected, as Richard would have to adapt his family's values and resources for an eventual journey northward to Kingston, Upper Canada, where his family would start anew.

In 1755, Richard may have seen himself as a devoted British subject raising a Loyalist family, but history was about to test that loyalty. Henry's early years unfolded against a backdrop of increasingly charged colonial sentiment—a formative time that would ultimately shape him and his siblings as they witnessed both war and revolution, upheavals that would guide the course of the entire Cartwright family for generations to come.

AT 38 YEARS OLD, RICHARD Cartwright welcomed another son, also named Richard, born on February 2, 1759, in Albany. The birth of his second son marked a significant moment for the family as they were continuing to grow amidst a world of uncertainty.

A Growing Family in Tumultuous Times

The late 1750s were a period of intense upheaval as the French and Indian War had already deepened its effects on colonial life. The Cartwrights' household, already with a growing number of children, likely felt the pressure of a strained and divided society. As a Loyalist, Richard would have been conscious that his family was increasingly surrounded by those who were displeased with British authority and imperial policies. Despite these tensions, the arrival of his second son may have given Richard renewed purpose, strengthening his commitment to securing a future for his children under British rule.

Richard's Legacy

Naming his son Richard would have been a reflection of his own sense of continuity and legacy. It was a name passed down to ensure that his lineage would carry on, with the younger Richard expected to carry the Cartwright name and, perhaps, the family's strong allegiance to the Crown. Richard would have likely seen this child as another opportunity to mold a future generation who would follow his example, a symbol of resilience in an increasingly unstable environment.

Family Life During the War

For Richard and Joanna, the continued expansion of their family was both a blessing and a challenge. Joanna had already raised multiple children through the tumult of war, and the responsibilities of motherhood were compounded as the Cartwrights' family grew larger. The strain of managing a large household in such times of conflict could not have been easy, but Richard would have provided what stability he could through his role in the community and his support for the British cause.

The younger Richard's early years would have unfolded amid growing tensions, as the British and French colonial forces clashed not only on the battlefield but also in the minds of the people. This environment would have influenced the way young Richard, and his siblings, understood their identity as Loyalists. With a father firmly in favor of British rule, the Cartwright children would have been raised in an atmosphere where allegiance to the Crown was deeply ingrained.

Richard's Growing Understanding of His World

As Richard Cartwright II grew older, he would likely come to understand the complexities of the world around him—recognizing that his family's status as Loyalists would make them both part of a privileged class and also set them on a trajectory of increasing alienation from their neighbors who supported the Patriot cause. In his early years, Richard was likely sheltered from the growing tensions, but as the conflict between Britain and the colonies deepened, the Cartwrights would find themselves at the center of a movement that would soon escalate into a full-scale revolution.

Challenges Ahead

With the birth of his second son, Richard Cartwright would have felt the pressure of an uncertain future. The French and Indian War was only a prelude to the larger conflicts that were about to unfold. The Cartwright family would, within a few short years, face the reality of the American Revolution—a conflict that would separate Loyalists from Patriots and lead them on a difficult journey to Kingston, Upper Canada.

The birth of his son Richard in 1759 would have been a moment of joy amidst the uncertainty, but also a reminder that the Cartwright family's future was tethered to the winds of war. For Richard and Joanna, the arrival of their son was an affirmation of their hope for a better future, even if that future was about to be shaped by tumultuous events.

---

AT 39 YEARS OLD, RICHARD Cartwright experienced the dawn of the Industrial Revolution, a profound shift in the world that began in the late 18th century, primarily in Britain, and slowly spread to the rest of Europe and the Americas. While this revolution did not immediately reach the rural colonies of North America, it nonetheless laid the foundation for vast economic and social changes that would have a significant impact on Richard's life and the future of his family.

The Industrial Revolution: A Changing Landscape

By the late 1750s and into the 1760s, the Industrial Revolution was gathering momentum in Britain, marked by significant advancements in manufacturing, machinery, and technology. Innovations such as the steam engine, mechanized cotton spinning, and improvements in transportation were transforming industries and the very nature of work. These changes would take decades to impact the colonies in North America directly, but the effects were already being felt in terms of trade, commerce, and the growing integration of global markets.

While Richard Cartwright was primarily focused on his life as a Loyalist and his growing family in Albany, these larger trends in Europe and beyond were beginning to reshape the world around him. His position as a merchant and a landowner meant he was involved in a rapidly changing economic environment that would soon be affected by these technological advancements. It is likely that, in his late 30s, Richard would have been aware of these shifts, even if they were not immediately affecting his day-to-day life in the same way they were in more industrialized parts of the world.

Economic Shifts and Opportunities

The Industrial Revolution brought with it the rise of factory-based manufacturing and the increasing use of mechanization in production. For a landowner like Richard, this could have signaled changes in the way goods were produced and transported. The increasing reliance on coal and steam power meant that goods could be made more efficiently and in larger quantities, which would eventually disrupt traditional artisan and craft-based production.

While the revolution would take time to reach colonial America, some of its effects were already being felt in the form of changing trade patterns. British imports and exports were increasing, and the expansion of the British empire through trade networks opened up new opportunities—and new challenges—for merchants like Richard.

As a Loyalist, Richard might have viewed the rise of industrialism in Britain as a sign of strength, solidifying his allegiance to the Crown and the established systems of power and commerce that supported it. This sense of optimism about Britain's future could have been a source of reassurance as political tensions began to grow within the colonies.

## The Impact of New Technology

Although Richard Cartwright's life in Albany was still largely agricultural, the new wave of technology and industrial advancements began to shape the future of the economy in North America. The introduction of steamships, railroads, and mass production techniques in the coming decades would lead to a transformation of transportation and trade networks. For Richard, this meant that his position as a merchant and landowner would eventually be impacted by these innovations, requiring him to adapt his business strategies to an evolving market.

By the time Richard was in his 40s, the effects of industrialization would begin to take hold, even in more rural areas like Albany. The increased demand for raw materials such as timber, iron, and cotton would mean more opportunities for landowners and merchants to supply the growing industries, but it would also lead to changes in the social and economic structure of the colonies.

## A Shifting World for His Children

As Richard's children grew older, they would find themselves coming of age in a world rapidly changing under the influence of industrialization. The older Richard Cartwright would likely begin to see his sons and daughters inherit a different world than the one he grew up in. The economic opportunities would shift, as new industries and the rise of capitalism began to reshape society in ways that had not been seen before.

By the time Richard's second son, Richard II, was of age, he would likely encounter a rapidly expanding world of factories, steamships, and railroads. The traditional agricultural way of life that Richard had known would begin to give way to more urban, industrialized environments where his descendants might seek opportunities.

Richard's Role as a Loyalist

Amid these global changes, Richard Cartwright's firm stance as a Loyalist might have placed him at odds with the more revolutionary currents developing in the colonies. The political tensions between Britain and the American colonies were escalating, and Richard's continued loyalty to the Crown would have been tested by the growing calls for independence. Despite this, Richard might have seen the industrial boom in Britain as a reason to stand by his allegiance to the British empire, convinced that the strength of the British economy and its global influence could provide security and prosperity for his family.

The changes brought by the Industrial Revolution would, in time, affect not only the world in which Richard Cartwright lived but also the lives of his children and grandchildren. However, in 1759, when Richard was 39, the full effects of these transformations were still on the horizon. The world was on the brink of a new age, and the Cartwright family, firmly planted in the world of colonial America, would soon find itself navigating both the industrial changes and the social upheaval of the American Revolution.

RICHARD CARTWRIGHT'S allegiance as a Loyalist during the American Revolution significantly influenced the course of his life, ultimately leading him to settle in Kingston, Ontario, after the war.

Loyalist Allegiance and the American Revolution

As the American Revolution unfolded in the 1770s, Richard Cartwright, along with many other loyalists, remained steadfast in his loyalty to the British Crown. This put him in opposition to the burgeoning revolutionary movement in the American colonies. As tensions escalated between the colonies and Britain, Richard's position would have been increasingly difficult, especially in a town like Albany, which was at the heart of colonial resistance.

Loyalists such as Cartwright faced increasing persecution during the Revolution. In Albany, many Loyalists found themselves marginalized, their property confiscated or damaged by revolutionary forces. The decision to remain loyal to the Crown during the conflict was not an easy one, as it often led to personal sacrifice, and it was a decision that led many to eventually leave the United States following the Revolution.

Post-Revolutionary Years: Settlement in Kingston, Ontario

After the war ended in 1783, the Treaty of Paris formally recognized the independence of the United States. However, this left many Loyalists in a precarious position. Loyalists were often faced with the loss of property and social standing in their former American homes, and many sought refuge in the remaining British colonies. In what became known as the "Loyalist migration," tens of thousands of Loyalists relocated to Canada, particularly to what are now the provinces of Ontario, New Brunswick, and Nova Scotia.

For Richard Cartwright, the decision to settle in Kingston, Ontario, was likely motivated by both a desire for safety and a fresh start. Kingston, located on the shores of Lake Ontario, was strategically important and had been a key military post during the war. By the time Richard arrived, Kingston was growing into a significant military and administrative center under British control.

Life in Kingston

Arriving in Kingston in the late 1780s, Richard would have witnessed the town's transformation from a military outpost to a developing settlement. Kingston had served as the headquarters of the British Army's forces in Upper Canada, and many Loyalists who had supported Britain during the war were granted land in the area as a reward for their loyalty. As a merchant and landowner, Richard likely found opportunities in the growing town, which was becoming a hub for trade and commerce in the region.

Kingston was a thriving community by the 1790s, with its strategic location offering access to both the St. Lawrence River and the Great Lakes. The town became an important port for British goods, and Richard's background as a merchant would have allowed him to engage in trade, supplying goods to both the military and civilian populations in the region.

Family Life in Kingston

Richard and his family would have settled in Kingston along with many other Loyalists, creating a new community of families displaced by the Revolution. Kingston offered safety and opportunities for economic growth, but it also required adaptation. Richard's sons and daughters, including John, Richard II, and Susannah, would have grown up in a town that was marked by both military presence and the rapid changes of a newly established British colony.

Richard's loyalty to the British Crown continued to play a role in his life in Kingston. The city's leadership was largely made up of those who had supported Britain during the American Revolution. Loyalists like Richard were integral to shaping the character of the new colonies in Canada. His role as a Loyalist likely gave him social standing and influence within the community, particularly in Kingston's more established Loyalist circles.

Richard's Legacy

Richard Cartwright's decision to remain loyal to the British Crown during the American Revolution, and to settle in Kingston after the war, positioned him as a key figure in the early history of Upper Canada. As a merchant, landowner, and family man, he contributed to the development of Kingston as an important center of trade and administration. His experience as a Loyalist, both during the war and in his later life, would have had a lasting impact on his descendants, shaping their lives in a newly formed Canada that was deeply rooted in its British heritage.

By the time of his death in 1794, Richard had seen Kingston grow from a strategic outpost into a burgeoning settlement, and his family's role as part of the Loyalist diaspora helped lay the groundwork for the future of Upper Canada.

AT 62 YEARS OLD, RICHARD Cartwright would have been living in Kingston, Ontario, a growing settlement in Upper Canada, as the world experienced the dawn of significant technological advancements. The year was 1783, and a momentous event took place in France that would capture the attention of people around the world: the first successful flight of a hot air balloon.

On June 4, 1783, the Montgolfier brothers, Joseph-Michel and Jacques-Étienne, launched the first manned flight in a hot air balloon in Annonay, France. The flight was brief but groundbreaking, marking the first time humans flew through the air using hot air as the lifting force. This invention would pave the way for future developments in aviation.

For Richard, who had lived through the Revolutionary War and witnessed the dramatic changes in his world, this invention was a symbol of the rapid progress that was taking place not just in Europe, but globally. While Kingston itself was still a small settlement in the late 18th century, the world beyond Canada was moving toward new frontiers of technology, exploration, and innovation. The concept of human flight, once thought impossible, was now becoming a reality, and this would have intrigued Richard and others in his community.

Though it's unlikely that Richard would have had direct contact with the Montgolfier brothers' work, the news of such a breakthrough would have traveled across the Atlantic and could have reached the small Loyalist community in Kingston, perhaps through newspapers or word of mouth. As a man who had seen the American Revolution, the formation of new governments, and the settlement of Upper Canada, Richard may have viewed this new invention with a sense of awe at how the world was changing. It would not have been far from his imagination to think about the potential future of this technology—what it might mean for trade, exploration, or even the military.

For Richard Cartwright, the success of the hot air balloon flight marked the beginning of a new era of exploration and possibility, both literally and figuratively. As a Loyalist who had seen the geopolitical landscape of the Americas shift dramatically, the idea that humans might one day fly through the air would have seemed as extraordinary and transformative as the events of his own life.

———————————

RICHARD CARTWRIGHT I passed away on October 23, 1794, at the age of 74, in Kingston, Upper Canada, a town that had become home to many Loyalists who had fled the upheaval of the American Revolution. By the time of his death, Kingston was evolving into an important military and administrative center for the British Empire in North America, and it was a growing community of former Loyalists like Richard who had helped lay its foundations.

As a man who had lived through the turbulent years of the French and Indian War, the American Revolution, and the Loyalist migration to Canada, Richard's life had been marked by dramatic change. By the time of his passing, Upper Canada (later Ontario) was a place of stability for many former colonists, though it was still in its formative years. The British government had established a presence in the area, and the town of Kingston was becoming a key point in the British military system.

Richard's burial in St. Paul's Churchyard, Kingston, was likely a fitting end for a man who had been deeply connected to the early development of the region. St. Paul's Anglican Church was one of the first churches built in Kingston, and it held great significance for the community, especially among the Loyalists. Many of those who had settled in Kingston after the American Revolution were of Anglican faith, and the church would have served as both a place of worship and a community hub.

As a prominent Loyalist, Richard's legacy lived on through his children and his contributions to the growth of Kingston. His life, marked by both personal and political challenges, was intertwined with the transformation of the region from a war-torn frontier into a thriving British settlement. His burial in St. Paul's Churchyard symbolized the end of one chapter in the history of Kingston and the Loyalist presence in Canada, even as the town itself continued to grow into the future.

HERE'S A GENEALOGY travel itinerary that traces the life and legacy of Richard Cartwright I, focusing on his journey from Colton, Staffordshire, to Kingston, Upper Canada:

**Day 1: Colton, Staffordshire, England**

Morning:

• Start at St. Mary's Church: Visit the parish church in Colton, where Richard Cartwright I would have been baptized and where the community gathered for worship and social events.

Afternoon:

• Explore Colton Village: Walk through the village to get a sense of the rural life in early 18th-century England. Visit local landmarks and imagine the agricultural lifestyle that dominated the area.

Evening:

• Stay in a Local Inn: Enjoy the hospitality of a traditional English inn, reflecting on the early years of Richard's life in Colton.

**Day 2: Stafford, Staffordshire, England**

Morning:

• Travel to Stafford: Visit the Staffordshire County Museum to learn about the broader historical context of the region during the Georgian period.

Afternoon:

• Explore Stafford Town Centre: Walk through the historic town center, visiting sites such as the Ancient High House and Stafford Castle.

Evening:

• Stay in Stafford: Enjoy the local cuisine and reflect on the economic and social landscape of the time.

**Day 3: Birmingham, England**

Morning:

• Travel to Birmingham: Visit the Birmingham Museum and Art Gallery to understand the early industrial developments that were beginning to take shape during Richard's lifetime.

Afternoon:

• Explore the Jewellery Quarter: Learn about the trades and crafts that were flourishing in Birmingham, which might have influenced families like the Cartwrights.

Evening:

• Stay in Birmingham: Experience the vibrant city life and consider the contrast between rural Colton and the growing urban centers.

**Day 4: London, England**

Morning:

• Travel to London: Visit the British Museum to explore exhibits on Georgian England and the Enlightenment.

Afternoon:

• Explore Historic London: Walk through areas such as Covent Garden and the Strand, visiting landmarks like St. Paul's Cathedral and the Tower of London.

Evening:

• Stay in London: Enjoy the cultural offerings of the capital city, reflecting on the broader context of Richard's early life.

**Day 5: Liverpool, England**

**Morning:**

• Travel to Liverpool: Visit the Merseyside Maritime Museum to learn about the port city's role in trade and emigration during the 18th century.

Afternoon:

• Explore the Albert Dock: Walk through the historic docklands, imagining the departure of families like the Cartwrights to the New World.

Evening:

• Stay in Liverpool: Enjoy the maritime atmosphere and consider the journey across the Atlantic.

**Day 6: Montreal, Quebec, Canada**

Morning:

• Fly to Montreal: Begin the Canadian leg of the journey, following the path of many Loyalists.

Afternoon:

• Visit the Château Ramezay: This historic site in Montreal offers insights into the Loyalist migration and settlement in Canada.

Evening:

• Explore Old Montreal: Walk through the historic streets and imagine the arrival of Loyalist families seeking refuge.

**Day 7: Amherst Island, Ontario**

Morning:

• Travel to Amherst Island: This island was a significant stop for many Loyalists on their way to Kingston. The ferry service from Millhaven Wharf to Stella Wharf on Amherst Island is a scenic and historically significant route

AFTERNOON:

• Explore Amherst Island: Visit local historical sites and learn about the Loyalist settlements on the island.

Evening:

• Stay on Amherst Island: Enjoy the peaceful surroundings and reflect on the journey of the Loyalists.

**Day 8: Kingston, Ontario**

Morning:

• Ferry to Kingston: Continue the journey to Kingston, where many Loyalists, including Richard Cartwright I, eventually settled.

Afternoon:

• Visit St. Paul's Anglican Churchyard: Pay respects at the final resting place of Richard Cartwright I and his wife, Joanna. Reflect on their contributions to the Loyalist community in Kingston.

Evening:

• Explore Kingston: Walk through the historic downtown area and visit sites like Fort Henry, which played a role in the defense of the region.

**Day 9: Kingston, Ontario**

Morning:

• Visit the United Empire Loyalist Heritage Centre and Park: Located in Adolphustown, near Kingston, this site offers a deep dive into the history and contributions of Loyalists in Canada.

Afternoon:

• Explore the Kingston Penitentiary: Learn about the history of the penitentiary and its connections to the early settlers of Kingston.

Evening:

• Stroll along the Waterfront: Enjoy the scenic views of Lake Ontario and reflect on the legacy of the Loyalists in Kingston.

**Day 10: Rideau Lakes, Ontario**

Morning:

• Drive to Rideau Lakes: This area is known for its beautiful landscapes and historical significance.

Afternoon:

• Explore the Rideau Canal: A UNESCO World Heritage Site, the canal was built by Loyalists and their descendants.

------

VISIT THE LOCKS AND learn about the engineering marvels of the time

<u>Loyalist Trails 2008-10 – UELAC</u>[1]

<hr>

EVENING:

• Relax by the Lakes: Enjoy the natural beauty and reflect on the journey of Richard Cartwright I and his family.

This itinerary offers a comprehensive journey through the historical sites and landscapes that shaped the lives of Richard Cartwright I and his descendants, providing a deeper understanding of their experiences and legacy.

1. https://uelac.ca/loyalist-trails/loyalist-trails-2008-10/

# ELIZABETH "BETSY" (ALGER) ADSIT[6]

In 1752, when Elizabeth "Betsy" Alger was born in Lyme, Connecticut, life in the American colonies was largely shaped by a blend of traditional European influences, the rise of colonial self-identity, and the onset of increasing tensions between the colonies and Britain.

Lyme, Connecticut, located along the picturesque Connecticut River, was a small but growing agricultural community. The economy of Lyme, like many other parts of New England, was largely based on farming, fishing, and shipbuilding, with many families working the land. Lyme was a coastal town, and seafaring was an important part of the local economy, with merchant ships and trade being key aspects of daily life. The 18th century was a time when many colonial towns were beginning to feel the influence of the rapidly expanding British Empire, which dominated global trade.

For Betsy's family, life in Lyme would have been one of relative comfort, as her father, Roger Alger III, was likely a part of the colonial elite, though still far from the wealth of large British landowners. Connecticut, like many New England colonies, was a center of trade, and families in towns like Lyme often enjoyed a modest level of prosperity from local industry, farming, and maritime pursuits.

Religious life was central in the early 18th century, with the Congregationalist church being the dominant faith in much of New England, including Connecticut. Like many New England towns, Lyme would have had a strong Puritan influence, and it would have been expected that families adhered to the moral and religious codes of the community.

Betsy was born into a time when American colonists were still largely loyal to Britain, though by 1752, the colonies had already begun to chafe under British rule. The tensions that would eventually lead to the American Revolution were already beginning to take shape, with issues like taxation, representation, and colonial governance becoming increasingly contentious. By the time Betsy was a child, debates around freedom and colonial rights were beginning to stir, and these events would shape the world she grew up in.

For a young woman like Betsy, much of her life would have revolved around the home and family. Women were primarily responsible for running households, managing domestic affairs, and raising children, though in communities like Lyme, women also often had roles in local commerce, crafts, and sometimes even politics. Betsy would likely have been raised with a strong sense of duty to her family and community, with an education focused on practical skills such as reading, sewing, and homemaking.

In the larger context of history, Betsy's birth in 1752 also positioned her as a contemporary of key figures in American history, including George Washington, Benjamin Franklin, and others whose actions would shape the fate of the colonies. The future revolutionary ideals of liberty and independence would loom large on the horizon, and though she was born into a time of relative peace, the world she would grow into would be one of profound political and social upheaval.

---

WHEN ELIZABETH "BETSY" Alger was just 1 year old in 1754, the French and Indian War began, marking a significant turning point in colonial American history. This conflict, which lasted until 1763, was a part of the larger Seven Years' War between Britain and France, fought across multiple continents, but it was particularly crucial in North America. The war was fought between the British colonies and their Native American allies against the French and their own indigenous partners.

For Betsy's family in Lyme, Connecticut, the impact of the war would have been felt indirectly at first, though the war's influence on the colonies as a whole would grow over time. Lyme, located on the coast, was part of the broader New England region that was deeply involved in the war's economic and military repercussions. While the fighting itself largely took place in the Ohio River Valley and along the frontier, the war's consequences would shape the lives of colonists across the continent.

During the French and Indian War, tensions between the British colonists and the Native American tribes allied with the French would have heightened the sense of insecurity in the colonies. Settlers in areas farther from the coast were at risk of attacks, and the war increased the need for military readiness and defense. While Lyme itself may not have experienced direct battles, there was widespread fear of raids and skirmishes, as well as a growing awareness of the contested nature of land and resources in North America.

The war also had profound economic effects. The British government heavily taxed the colonies to fund the war effort, and the colonists were increasingly unhappy about having to bear the financial burden without representation in Parliament. This sense of injustice, along with the resentment over British interference in colonial affairs, began to foster a growing sense of colonial identity and a desire for self-determination. The taxes and laws passed by the British government, such as the Stamp Act and the Townshend Acts, were among the grievances that would later lead to the American Revolution.

For Betsy's family, the economic strain would likely have been felt, though Lyme was a prosperous area, and her family may have been somewhat insulated from the most severe impacts of the war. However, the war's end in 1763, with the Treaty of Paris, resulted in Britain gaining significant territory in North America, but also put the colonies under greater control of the British government. The taxes levied on the colonies to pay for the war's expenses, along with the encroachment on colonial autonomy, would set the stage for the revolutionary ideas that were beginning to take root in the years that followed.

As Betsy grew older, she would have witnessed the increased tensions and unrest that followed the French and Indian War, and the lasting effects of the war on the colonies, including the rising resentment against British rule, which would eventually culminate in the American Revolution.

WHEN ELIZABETH "BETSY" Alger was 2 years old in 1755, her family welcomed her brother, Greenfield Alger, born in Lyme, Connecticut on May 18. The year 1755 was a tumultuous time in colonial America, as it marked the escalation of the French and Indian War, a conflict that had begun the previous year. This war would shape much of Betsy's early childhood, and the birth of her brother occurred during a period when tensions between the British colonists and the French were intensifying, particularly in the Ohio River Valley.

In Lyme, the war's effects would have been felt mainly through its economic and social disruptions, even though the town itself was not a direct battleground. As a coastal community in Connecticut, Lyme's residents were closely tied to maritime trade, and any disruptions in trade routes or military actions along the coast would have had economic consequences. There may also have been heightened anxiety about possible raids or attacks by the French or their Native American allies, who had established strong partnerships with various tribes in the region.

In 1755, the British were undertaking military campaigns in North America, and the year saw significant military developments. One of the most notable events was the British defeat at the Battle of the Monongahela, which resulted in the death of General Edward Braddock. This loss, along with several other setbacks for the British, contributed to the growing frustration and division between the colonists and the British military leadership, especially in how the colonies were being managed during the war.

For Betsy's parents, Roger Alger III and Elizabeth Greenfield, the birth of their son Greenfield likely brought both joy and added responsibility. Like many families of the time, they would have had to manage the effects of the war on their daily lives, balancing the challenges of military conflict, economic pressures, and a growing sense of unrest within the colonies. The birth of a son was an important event, as male children were seen as vital to the family line and the continuation of their agricultural lifestyle, which would have been the foundation of the Alger family's livelihood.

As Betsy grew older, she would have witnessed the unfolding consequences of the war, especially as British troops continued to fight the French and their Native American allies across North America. She would have also seen the growing strain between the colonists and the British government, which was imposing taxes and laws that would lead to increased discontent. Her brother Greenfield, as he matured, would have been caught in the middle of these tensions as well, especially as the colonies neared the revolutionary period in the years to come.

———————

WHEN ELIZABETH "BETSY" Alger was 6 years old, her father, Roger Alger III, passed away in Lyme, Connecticut, on August 2, 1759. This would have been a significant and difficult moment in Betsy's early childhood. The loss of a father at such a young age likely had a profound impact on her, especially given the social and economic challenges of the time.

In 1759, the French and Indian War was still ongoing, and the war's effects were felt even in relatively peaceful New England towns like Lyme. Roger Alger III's death would have left his family to cope without his presence, particularly in a time when the male head of a household typically played a crucial role in managing the family's economic affairs, farm, and community responsibilities. The loss of a father was particularly hard in a colonial family, as men were often the primary breadwinners, and their deaths could destabilize a household financially and emotionally.

Elizabeth's mother, Elizabeth Greenfield Alger, would have had to step into a more central role in supporting the family. At the time, widows often faced difficult circumstances, especially if their husbands had not left behind a substantial estate or financial means. Women like Elizabeth Greenfield were expected to raise children, maintain the household, and manage the affairs of the farm or property, all while navigating the hardships of a widowhood that was often marked by social and economic challenges.

Betsy and her brother, Greenfield, would have grown up without the strong paternal figure that might have been expected in their early lives, and their mother's resilience would have been key in helping them navigate this change. With her father's death, Betsy would have seen firsthand the challenges that women faced in a patriarchal society where they were often left to manage the family in the absence of a man. The death of Roger Alger may also have affected the family's financial situation, depending on how much property or wealth he had left behind, and how well the family was able to maintain their lifestyle during this time of upheaval.

In the broader context of the war, by 1759 the French and Indian War was nearing its end. The British had gained significant victories in Canada and the Great Lakes, and the tide was turning in favor of the British colonists. However, the war was still a source of great tension in the colonies, and Roger Alger's death could have been influenced by the strained circumstances of the time, including war-related stress or sickness that might have affected the community. This period also marked growing discontent with the British rule, which would become increasingly significant in the coming decades.

Though Betsy was young when her father passed, she would have likely been aware of the changes in her family dynamic. Over the next few years, she would have experienced the shifting social and economic landscapes of Lyme, with her mother managing the household and both children growing up amidst the lasting effects of the war and the changing world of colonial America.

AT 19 YEARS OLD, ELIZABETH "Betsy" Alger married Ebenezer Adsit in Lyme, Connecticut, in 1772. This was a significant life event for Betsy, marking her transition from adolescence to adulthood in the midst of a rapidly changing and tumultuous time in colonial America.

In 1772, life in the colonies was filled with growing tensions between the British and American colonists, though the Revolutionary War had not yet broken out. The decade leading up to the Revolution saw increasing unrest as the British imposed taxes and laws that many colonists found unjust. While Lyme, being a smaller town in Connecticut, was not at the center of political conflict like Boston or New York, the events leading to the American Revolution would have been a source of discussion and division within the community.

Marriage at 19 was not unusual for young women in colonial America, especially in rural or small-town areas like Lyme. It was common for women to marry in their late teens or early twenties, and marriage was often seen as a key part of a woman's life, particularly for those from established families. Betsy's marriage to Ebenezer Adsit would have been a significant social and familial event. Ebenezer Adsit was likely from a well-established family in Lyme as well, which would have helped solidify their position in the local community.

The year 1772 was a time when families were still primarily agricultural, and Betsy would have expected to manage a household, help on the farm or in family businesses, and begin raising children. The economic landscape, while not as strained as it would become during the Revolutionary War, was still challenging for most families. For Betsy, marriage was not only a personal commitment but also a partnership that would likely have provided a sense of security during uncertain times. Ebenezer, like many men of the era, would have worked as a farmer, tradesman, or in another local occupation to support his family.

Although not yet involved in the broader political movements of the Revolution, Betsy would have been surrounded by a climate of growing dissent toward British rule. In Connecticut, as in much of New England, many people were aligning themselves with the patriot cause, while others remained loyal to the Crown. It is likely that Betsy's marriage to Ebenezer Adsit brought her into closer contact with his family and his social circles, and the political climate would have affected the decisions they made as a couple.

The next few years would see Betsy's life shift toward raising a family. Within the next few years, she and Ebenezer would likely have begun having children, as was typical in colonial America. Their marriage and family life would have been shaped by the same societal pressures that were pushing toward greater independence, as well as the constant challenges of life in an era marked by instability and political change. The birth of their children would have marked another phase in Betsy's life, and she would have become deeply involved in the daily duties of homemaking, child-rearing, and managing the household, all while the world around her began to change dramatically as the Revolutionary War approached.

As Betsy settled into her role as a wife and mother, she would likely have been part of the growing wave of American women who became more politically engaged during the Revolution, whether through formal means or in the more private spheres of the home, where ideas of liberty, independence, and self-governance were discussed among families.

AT 21 YEARS OLD, IN 1774, Elizabeth "Betsy" Alger would have been living in a time of intense political upheaval. As the First Continental Congress convened in Philadelphia that year, the atmosphere in the colonies was charged with rising tensions. Colonists were increasingly frustrated with British policies, particularly the Coercive Acts (known in America as the Intolerable Acts), which had been imposed in response to the Boston Tea Party in 1773.

Although Betsy was living in Lyme, Connecticut, far from the political centers of the rebellion, the news and sentiments of the time would have reached her through local gatherings, newspapers, and the influence of her family and community. It is likely that debates and discussions about the colonies' growing defiance toward Britain were taking place in Lyme as well, as many Connecticut colonists were firmly against British rule.

As delegates met for the First Continental Congress in September 1774, they discussed how to respond to the Intolerable Acts and the escalating tensions between the colonies and the Crown. One of the first steps they took was to adopt a unified stance, sending a petition of grievances to King George III, and also agreeing to stop all trade with Britain. The Congress also agreed to meet again if their demands were not addressed. This marked a significant step toward unity among the colonies and was an early stage in the development of the American Revolution.

Though Betsy was not directly involved in the political actions taking place in Philadelphia, these developments would have had a profound impact on her life. At the time, she was likely focused on her own personal life as a wife and potentially preparing for motherhood, but the broader political events happening in the colonies could not have been ignored. News of the Continental Congress and the growing unrest would have spread quickly, and Betsy would have heard about it through local leaders, town meetings, and her social circles.

Betsy's family, like many in Connecticut, may have had strong opinions on the matter. Connecticut was a largely patriotic colony, and many residents were deeply involved in the Revolutionary cause. If Betsy and her husband, Ebenezer Adsit, were loyal to the Crown, this would have created a tension for them in a region that leaned toward independence. This period would have been one of personal and societal upheaval, as loyalists like Betsy and Ebenezer found themselves at odds with their neighbors, who were increasingly siding with the revolutionary cause.

While Betsy may not have been directly participating in political meetings or actions, her life was undoubtedly shaped by the decisions being made in the Continental Congress. The uncertainty and conflict of the era were bound to affect her, from her community relationships to the future of her family. As the year went on, and the colonies moved closer to rebellion, Betsy would have had to navigate a complex world where political allegiance could divide families, friends, and neighbors.

IN 1774, AT THE AGE of 21, Betsy Alger welcomed her first child, a son named Elijah, in Lyme, Connecticut. This was a time of great change in the American colonies, as tensions with Britain escalated, and the foundations for the American Revolution were being laid. While Betsy was focused on motherhood and managing her household, the events unfolding around her would certainly have shaped her and her family's future.

Given that she was living in Lyme, a town in a region known for its strong patriot sentiments, Betsy would have likely been surrounded by people who were deeply involved in the movement toward independence. Lyme itself was a coastal town, and many of its residents were active in the Revolutionary cause. Her husband, Ebenezer Adsit, and other members of her community would have been discussing the political developments that were sweeping through the colonies, especially the actions of the Continental Congress and the colonial protests against British rule.

As Betsy nursed her newborn son and adjusted to the demands of motherhood, she might have also been acutely aware of the increasing pressure on colonial families as the Revolution drew nearer. The birth of Elijah, her first child, would have introduced a new layer of responsibility for her, as raising a child during such uncertain times would have been fraught with challenges. The family would have had to deal with not just the typical struggles of child-rearing but also the larger concerns of a nation on the brink of war.

For Betsy, the arrival of Elijah might have been both a personal joy and a reminder of the uncertain future facing the American colonies. As the colonies moved toward armed resistance, mothers like Betsy were faced with the possibility of sending their sons into the conflict, an idea that may have been especially poignant for her, as she navigated her new role as a mother in a world that was rapidly changing. It was a time of personal and national transformation, and her life was now intertwined with the fate of a nation on the cusp of revolution.

As the year went on and the American Revolution began in earnest, Betsy would have witnessed her town and family grow even more divided. With Lyme's strong Patriot influence, Betsy's Loyalist sympathies may have created tension with neighbors and even her own extended family, whose views on independence were likely more radical. Raising Elijah in the midst of all this turmoil would have been challenging, and Betsy would have had to make difficult decisions about how to protect her family and navigate the growing conflict between the Loyalists and the Patriots.

Her son, born into a time of rebellion, would grow up in an America on the verge of fundamental change, and Betsy would likely have played a central role in guiding him through the complexities of a divided country.

AS A PATRIOT, EBENEZER would have supported the cause for independence, which would have placed Betsy in a unique position. As a mother to Elijah, Betsy would have navigated the complex political landscape that divided families, communities, and even close relatives during the Revolution. With her husband aligned with the Patriot cause, it's likely that their household was more sympathetic to the fight for independence.

Betsy would have been affected by the changes sweeping through Lyme and Connecticut, both as a mother and as the wife of someone with strong ties to the revolutionary cause. There could have been tension within her family, particularly if she had any Loyalist relatives or connections. As was the case for many during the Revolution, the political divisions would have made everyday life challenging, as the loyalties of neighbors and even extended family members could create friction.

Betsy's personal and family life would have been shaped by these turbulent times. While she focused on raising Elijah, she might have also been supporting her husband's decisions, perhaps by hosting or attending local meetings or assisting with the care of soldiers or militia members, who would have been part of the Patriot cause. The Adsit family's experience would have been deeply intertwined with the larger events unfolding around them, and Betsy's role as a mother in a family that supported independence would have made her more acutely aware of the sacrifices required in times of war.

The birth of Elijah in 1774 would have come at the start of this tumultuous period, and Betsy would likely have been concerned for his future, knowing that the Revolution would bring enormous changes. Whether Betsy took on a more active role in supporting the Patriot cause or kept to a more traditional role at home, the Revolution would have undeniably shaped her worldview, her family's choices, and the life she built with her husband. As Elijah grew, he would have been raised in a household that supported the cause of liberty, and Betsy's life would have reflected the courage and resilience of a woman living through one of the most transformative periods in American history.

---

BETSY ALGER WAS 32 years old when her daughter Hannah was born in Canaan, New York, on March 16, 1785. This marked the beginning of a new chapter in Betsy's life, as the United States was in the early years of its independence, following the conclusion of the American Revolution in 1783. Life in the post-Revolutionary War era was filled with both challenges and opportunities for a woman like Betsy, who had already lived through the tumult of war and now found herself raising a young family in a newly-formed nation.

By 1785, the political landscape was shifting as the United States moved from the Articles of Confederation to the drafting of the U.S. Constitution. The nation was grappling with its new identity and economic challenges, including the establishment of a stable government, trade issues, and the integration of former British colonies into a cohesive whole. These developments would have shaped the context in which Betsy raised her children, particularly her young daughter Hannah.

Betsy's life would have been influenced by the changes in the community around her, including the establishment of post-war norms and institutions. The early years of the Republic brought opportunities for land expansion, but there were also remnants of old colonial challenges. With a new generation being raised, like Hannah, it was a time of rebuilding, not just politically, but socially and economically. The country was seeking its place on the world stage, and Betsy, now in her thirties, would have witnessed how the Revolution had shaped her generation's attitudes toward government, liberty, and the future.

Betsy's role as a mother during this time likely saw a blending of traditional family values with the ideals of a republic. Raising Hannah in an environment where the revolution was still a fresh memory, Betsy would have seen the importance of instilling values of liberty and independence in her children. They were part of a new generation—one that would grow up with the opportunity to define the country's future.

Hannah's birth in 1785 also symbolized a new era for Betsy, one where the nation was healing from the Revolutionary War but still facing the challenges of building a new, unified country. While Betsy navigated motherhood in a time of political flux, she likely embraced the hopes and dreams of a brighter future for her children, including Hannah, in a nation that had just begun to find its footing after a hard-fought revolution.

AT 38 YEARS OLD, BETSY Alger lived through the passage of the Bill of Rights in 1791. This landmark event, which marked the first ten amendments to the United States Constitution, secured individual freedoms and became a defining moment in the formation of the new nation. For Betsy, this was a time when the ideals of liberty and personal rights, central to the Revolution, were being enshrined in law, shaping the social and political landscape around her.

As a woman in the late 18th century, Betsy would have experienced a shift in the recognition of rights, even though women's rights were not yet a focal point in the political sphere. The Bill of Rights guaranteed freedoms such as speech, religion, and the press, as well as protections against unreasonable searches and seizures. These principles reflected the core values that motivated the American Revolution, and Betsy, like many of her contemporaries, likely saw them as vital to the progress of the nation.

At this point in her life, Betsy had already borne children and was raising her family in a new country that was trying to define itself. The passing of the Bill of Rights would have made her more aware of the emerging political debates of the time, even if she was not directly involved in them. The protection of property rights, the right to a fair trial, and freedom of speech would have resonated with her, especially as a mother and homemaker concerned with the future of her children, including her young daughter, Hannah, who was growing up in a nation in transition.

Though women did not yet have full participation in the political process, the changes brought about by the Bill of Rights helped lay the groundwork for future generations, including the eventual push for women's rights. Betsy's perspective as a woman living through the founding moments of the United States would have shaped how she viewed her role in society, even if that role was still largely domestic and centered around her family and community.

In the broader context of the nation's development, the passage of the Bill of Rights meant that Betsy was witnessing the establishment of legal and civil protections that would define American governance for generations. As she continued to raise her children, Betsy likely took comfort in the promises of liberty and justice, even as she navigated the limitations that women of her time faced. The values enshrined in the Bill of Rights would continue to influence the course of her life, as well as the future lives of her children, including her daughter Hannah, who would come of age in a nation where the ideals of freedom and personal rights were taking root.

***

AT 39 YEARS OLD, BETSY Alger gave birth to her daughter, Polly, in Canaan, New York, on September 15, 1792. This was a time when the new United States was still finding its footing after the

Revolutionary War and the passage of the Bill of Rights just a year prior. Betsy, now a mother of several children, was living in an evolving nation, and her life, though still grounded in family and community, was shaped by the changes and challenges of the post-Revolutionary era.

The 1790s were a transformative time for the United States, with the young republic still defining its political identity and navigating issues of federal power and states' rights. Betsy's family, having experienced the Revolutionary War, was likely attuned to the shifting political climate. For Betsy, life in the early 1790s would have involved caring for her growing family, and she would have been invested in their futures in a nation that was struggling to create a stable government.

Polly's birth came during a time of significant political and economic growth for the new republic. While Betsy herself may not have been directly involved in political matters, the changes happening in the country would have had indirect impacts on her life, especially in terms of economic stability, laws, and the rights of individuals. The debates over the nation's financial systems, the influence of Alexander Hamilton's policies, and the growing divisions between Federalists and Democratic-Republicans may have been subjects of discussion among her husband and neighbors, even if Betsy herself remained focused on raising her children.

As a mother of now five children, Betsy was likely experiencing the stresses and joys of family life in the post-Revolutionary era. With the birth of Polly, Betsy had another child to care for, and her domestic duties would have been extensive, as she juggled household responsibilities and the needs of her growing family. While her husband was involved in the community and possibly politics, Betsy's primary role was as a mother and homemaker, ensuring the well-being of her children in a rapidly changing world.

Polly's birth also came at a time when women's roles in society were still largely defined by the domestic sphere. Though the ideals of liberty and personal freedoms were taking root with the Bill of Rights and early political changes, women's rights had not yet been a focus of the political establishment. Nevertheless, Betsy's life, as a mother of multiple children, would have been influenced by the evolving nature of American society, particularly as it pertained to family life and economic survival.

As Polly grew up, she would be raised in a nation where new political ideas about liberty and individual rights continued to shape the national identity. Betsy, as a mother, would undoubtedly pass on values of hard work, family, and resilience to her daughter, much as she had for her other children. Polly's life, shaped by the same struggles and opportunities of the early Republic, would be different from her mother's, but she would carry with her the legacy of Betsy's role in her family's history.

AT 62 YEARS OLD, ELIZABETH "Betsy" Alger passed away in Westbrook, Ontario, in 1815. Her life, spanning over six decades, had witnessed the transformation of both her personal world and the larger world around her. Born during the era of British colonial dominance in North America, Betsy had seen the fall of British rule and the rise of an independent United States, only to later settle in Canada, a new chapter in her journey as a Loyalist.

By the time of her death in 1815, much had changed in the world. The War of 1812, fought between the United States and Britain, was winding down, and the Treaty of Ghent was signed in December of that year, signaling peace between the warring nations. For Betsy, who had lived through the American Revolution as a Loyalist, this period of renewed conflict would have had deep personal significance. She may have reflected on the struggles and sacrifices of her earlier years, particularly in light of her family's commitment to the British crown and their eventual relocation to Upper Canada after the Revolution.

In 1815, life in Ontario was still difficult but full of promise for those who had settled there, particularly for Loyalists like Betsy and her family. The region was sparsely populated but growing steadily as more settlers arrived, often seeking land grants in the wake of their wartime loyalty. Westbrook, where Betsy spent her final years, would have been part of this growing settlement, though it was still far from the bustling urban centers like Kingston or Toronto. Her days would have been spent in a rural, agricultural lifestyle, focused on family, community, and the hard work of farming or household management.

Betsy's legacy, deeply rooted in her values as a mother and a Loyalist, would have carried through in the lives of her children. Her experience as a mother, wife, and survivor of tumultuous times shaped her as someone who lived through great political and social upheaval. While she had faced the hardships of early life, she had also known the rewards of a large family, and her children, having grown up in an era of relative peace, would carry her lessons forward into their own lives.

Her burial in the Cataraqui Cemetery in Kingston, Ontario, marked the end of her journey. This cemetery, one of the oldest in the region, holds the remains of many early settlers, and Betsy's resting place would have been among those who played a part in shaping Ontario's early history. Kingston itself, having been a Loyalist stronghold during and after the American Revolution, was a fitting final home for Betsy, whose loyalty to the British crown had been a defining feature of her life.

Her passing in 1815 came at a time when her legacy as a mother, a pioneer, and a Loyalist would continue to influence the generations that followed. While she may have lived out her final years in relative quiet in Westbrook, her story — intertwined with the larger story of the British Empire, the American Revolution, and the formation of Canada — remained an important part of the history of those who came before her.

———————

HERE'S A GENEALOGY travel itinerary that traces the life and legacy of Elizabeth "Betsy" Alger, focusing on her journey from Lyme, Connecticut, through the significant events of her life:

**Day 1: Lyme, Connecticut**

Morning:

• Start at the Lyme Historical Society: Visit the Florence Griswold Museum to learn about the history of Lyme and the colonial era during Betsy's early years.

Afternoon:

• Explore the Connecticut River: Take a scenic boat tour to understand the importance of the river in the local economy, including farming, fishing, and shipbuilding.

Evening:

• Walk through Historic Lyme: Stroll through the town, visiting landmarks and imagining the daily life of Betsy and her family in the 18th century.

**Day 2: New London, Connecticut**

Morning:

• Travel to New London: Visit the New London County Historical Society to explore exhibits on the colonial period and the French and Indian War.

Afternoon:

• Explore Fort Trumbull State Park: Learn about the fort's role in the defense of the region during the French and Indian War and the American Revolution.

Evening:

• Stay in New London: Enjoy the coastal atmosphere and reflect on the maritime heritage that shaped the lives of families like the Algers.

**Day 3: Hartford, Connecticut**

Morning:

• Travel to Hartford: Visit the Connecticut Historical Society to delve into the broader history of Connecticut during the 18th century.

Afternoon:

• Explore the Old State House: Learn about the political landscape of Connecticut and the growing tensions with Britain that Betsy would have witnessed.

Evening:

• Stay in Hartford: Experience the historic charm of the city and consider the impact of colonial governance on local communities.

**Day 4: Boston, Massachusetts**

Morning:

• Travel to Boston: Visit the Boston Tea Party Ships and Museum to understand the events leading up to the American Revolution.

Afternoon:

• Explore the Freedom Trail: Walk through historic sites such as Paul Revere's House and the Old North Church, reflecting on the revolutionary spirit that was growing during Betsy's lifetime.

Evening:

• Stay in Boston: Enjoy the vibrant city life and think about the broader context of the American colonies' push for independence.

**Day 5: Albany, New York**

Morning:

• Travel to Albany: Visit the Albany Institute of History & Art to learn about the colonial history of New York and its role in the French and Indian War.

Afternoon:

• Explore the Schuyler Mansion State Historic Site: Understand the lives of prominent colonial families and the political dynamics of the time.

Evening:

• Stay in Albany: Reflect on the connections between New England and New York during the colonial period.

**Day 6: Montreal, Quebec, Canada**

Morning:

• Fly to Montreal: Begin the Canadian leg of the journey, following the path of many families affected by the French and Indian War.

Afternoon:

• Visit the Château Ramezay: This historic site in Montreal offers insights into the colonial history and the impact of the war on the region.

Evening:

• Explore Old Montreal: Walk through the historic streets and imagine the colonial interactions between French and British settlers.

**Day 7: Westbrook, Ontario, Canada**

Morning:

• Travel to Westbrook: Visit the local historical sites and cemeteries to pay respects to Betsy Alger, who passed away here around 1815.

Afternoon:

• Explore the Loyalist Parkway: Drive along this scenic route, reflecting on the journey of Loyalists and their settlement in Canada.

Evening:

• Stay in Kingston: Enjoy the historic downtown area and visit sites like Fort Henry, which played a role in the defense of the region.

**Day 8: Kingston, Ontario**

Morning:

• Visit St. Paul's Anglican Churchyard: Pay respects at the final resting place of many early settlers and reflect on their contributions to the community.

Afternoon:

• Explore the United Empire Loyalist Heritage Centre and Park: Located in Adolphustown, near Kingston, this site offers a deep dive into the history and contributions of Loyalists in Canada.

Evening:

• Stroll along the Waterfront: Enjoy the scenic views of Lake Ontario and reflect on the legacy of the early settlers in Kingston.

**Day 9: Rideau Lakes, Ontario**

Morning:

• Drive to Rideau Lakes: This area is known for its beautiful landscapes and historical significance.

Afternoon:

• Explore the Rideau Canal: A UNESCO World Heritage Site, the canal was built by Loyalists and their descendants. Visit the locks and learn about the engineering marvels of the time.

Evening:

• Relax by the Lakes: Enjoy the natural beauty and reflect on the journey of Elizabeth "Betsy" Alger and her family.

# LEST WE FORGET

Volunteers are needed. Thank you so much for your help.

<u>St. Paul's Anglican Churchyard</u>[1]

<u>Cataraqui Cemetery</u>[2]

[1] https://www.wikitree.com/wiki/Forrester-2536

[2] https://www.wikitree.com/wiki/Forbes-7702

[3] https://www.wikitree.com/wiki/Sweeney-4969

[4] https://www.wikitree.com/wiki/Beasley-1185

[5] https://www.wikitree.com/wiki/Cartwright-1344

[6] https://www.wikitree.com/wiki/Alger-292

---

1. https://billiongraves.com/cemetery/St-Pauls-Anglican-Churchyard/322924/volunteer

2. https://billiongraves.com/cemetery/Cataraqui-Cemetery/266806/volunteer

# Don't miss out!

Visit the website below and you can sign up to receive emails whenever Angeline Gallant publishes a new book. There's no charge and no obligation.

https://books2read.com/r/B-A-QGSI-VBCIF

**BOOKS 2 READ**

Connecting independent readers to independent writers.

# Also by Angeline Gallant

**A Dragon's Diary**
Dreaming of Dragons

**Blood and Spirit Saga**
The Rising Wind

**Calling Her Heart**
Whisper of the Heart
No Turning Back
Forsake Me Not
Hear My Cry

**FORGET ME NOT**
Victoria, Ontario's Babies 1894 - 1895

**GENERATIONS OF THE VOLGA**
A Family's Legacy

**Guardian of the Heart**
Fallen Petals


**Keeper Of Secrets**
A Lady's Secret


**Kingston's Love Chronicles**
Springtime Promises


**Midnight's Awakening**
Heart of the Storm
Walking Through The Storm
Walking Through The Storm
Heart of the Storm


**Secrets of the Underworld**
Deklan's Dragons


**Tell My Story Collection**
Tell My Story: Germany 1851
Tell My Story: England 1852
Whispers From The Garrison Church

**The Dervock Legacy**
Echoes of Dervock


**The Grave Whisperer**
Cataraqui United Church Cemetery
Whispers of Kingston
Wedding Bells in Kingston, Ontario, Canada 1923
St. Paul's Anglican Churchyard Kingston, Ontario, Canada A-B
St. Paul's Anglican Churchyard, Kingston, Ontario, Canada C - D
St. Paul's Anglican Churchyard, Kingston, Ontario, Canada G - H
St. Paul's Anglican Churchyard, Kingston, Ontario, Canada J - N
St. Paul's Anglican Churchyard, Kingston, Ontario, Canada O - R
St. Paul's Anglican Churchyard, Kingston, Ontario, Canada S - T
St. Paul's Anglican Churchyard, Kingston, Ontario T - Z
Small Graveyards & Burial Grounds: Kingston, Ontario, Canada
Cataraqui United Church Cemetery 1
Cataraqui United Church Cemetery 2
Cataraqui United Church Cemetary 3
Cataraqui United Church Cemetery 4
Cataraqui United Church Cemetery 5
Beth Israel Cemetery
Cataraqui United Church Cemetery 6
Beneath the Surface: Echoes from Beth Israel Cemetery
Grave Tales: Discovering the Lives of Beth Israel


**The Timeless Veil**
Eternal Devotion

**The Wolf Whisperer Series**
Cry of a Warrior
Wolf Whisperer volumes 1 & 2
Endless White
The Wolf Whisperer volumes 1 & 2


**Timeless**
The Time Keeper's Sanctuary


**Timeless Whispers of Dervock Saga**
Secrets of Dervock


**Standalone**
Winds of Change vol 1-3


Watch for more at https://www.goodreads.com/author/show/
19703964.Angeline_Gallant.

# About the Author

Angeline Gallant traces her roots through generations of Old Stock Canadian heritage, her passion for genealogy as deep and enduring as the forests and fields her ancestors once walked. With a reverence for history and an eye for detail, she weaves stories from the fragments of lives left behind in letters, records, and weathered headstones.

An avid reader and devoted writer, Angeline brings the past to life with a curiosity for heraldry and a deep love for the landscapes that shaped her family's story. Each name and date she uncovers feels less like history and more like coming home, a familiar echo in the vast tapestry of time. For her, these stories are not forgotten—they live, breathing in the quiet spaces of memory and tradition, a testament to lives once lived, now eternal in the pages of her books.

Read more at https://www.goodreads.com/author/show/19703964.Angeline_Gallant.